THE
GRECO-ROMAN
TRADITION

MAJOR TRADITIONS OF WORLD CIVILIZATION
UNDER THE EDITORSHIP OF HAYDEN V. WHITE

THE
GRECO-ROMAN
TRADITION

HAYDEN V. WHITE

University of California at Los Angeles

HARPER & ROW, PUBLISHERS

NEW YORK, EVANSTON, SAN FRANCISCO, LONDON

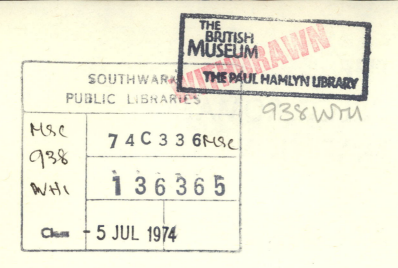

Sponsoring Editor: John G. Ryden
Project Editor: Christopher J. Kuppig
Designer: June Negrycz
Production Supervisor: Valerie Klima

THE GRECO-ROMAN TRADITION

Library of Congress Cataloging in Publication Data

White, Hayden V 1928–
     The Greco-Roman tradition.

     (Major traditions of world civilization)
     Bibliography: p.
     1. Civilization, Greek.   2. Rome—Civilization.
I. Title.   II. Series.
DF77.W53 1973   913.38′03   73–10069
ISBN 0–06–047064–X

CONTENTS

INTRODUCTION

Modern Western civilization can be conceived as an amalgam of three types of cultural traditions: barbarian (Germano-Celtic), oriental (Judaeo-Christian), and classical (Greco-Roman). This book is about the third type, the Greco-Roman. It is not, however, a history of the whole temporal career of this tradition, but only of its own original phase, from *ca.* 1,500 B.C. to *ca.* A.D. 400. More specifically this book does not pretend to cover (or even to mention) all of the most significant aspects of the civilization in which this tradition originated. It concentrates primarily on a single aspect of the tradition, humanism. And it organizes the histories of Greece and Rome around the problem of the rise and fall of the classical humanistic ideal.

Now, a number of terms used in the preceding paragraph require clarification. These are: tradition, classical, and humanism. If we can specify what we mean by these terms we shall be on our way to understanding the unique role played by Greco-Roman cultural ideals in the history of modern Western civilization.

First of all, tradition. The dictionaries tell us that this word derives from Latin *traditio*, a form of the verb *trādere*, which means "to hand over, to deliver." But the literal meaning of the term suggests that a tradition is a thing or object that can be passed from age to age without significant change, like a baton in a relay race. This is misleading. For a tradition is a complex of ideas that serves as a matrix into which different contents can be inserted and to which different experiences can be assimilated. It provides a kind of mental set that tells us not so much what to think but rather *how* to think and in what direction we should direct our thought in our efforts to make sense of the world. Successive ages in the history of Western civilization have perceived both the ancient Greeks and the ancient Romans differently. The "Greeks" of Shakespeare are hardly comparable to the "Greeks" of Nietzsche, and the "noble Romans" of Machiavelli bear little resemblance to the "noble Romans" of Montesquieu. What the Church Fathers of the fourth century A.D. found in the Greek and Roman "classics" was quite different from what either the Italian humanists of the fifteenth century or the French philosophes of the eighteenth-century Enlightenment found in them. But what makes all of these interpreters of classical civilization participants in the same *tradition* is the fact that they all accorded to that civilization a special status as a type, model, or ideal by appeal to which their own unique visions of reality could be sanctioned. Whatever differences we perceive between their several perceptions of Greco-Roman civilization, all of them honored that civilization as an exemplar of what a responsible humanity would aspire to. *They* made Greco-Roman civilization "classical" by their choice of it as a matrix within which to articulate their successive visions of reality. Their choices make up the tradition, just as much as the tradition determined the limits within which their conceptions of the world could be articulated. What a civilization is can be defined by what it does and what it aspires to, by the way it relates present projects to future goals. But it can also be defined by what it honors in its past as a model of what it ought to do and aspire to as well. A tradition forms the matrix in which memory and desire, practicality and ideality can be fused into a unified vision of historical becoming.

The term "classical" refers to the age or ideals that

any given civilization takes as the paradigm of the traditions that inform it. Different cultural traditions, different classics. For the Christian, the Apostolic age is the classical period par excellence, the New Testament the classic work by which all subsequent expressions of Christian faith are to be measured. For the Jew, the classical period may be the time of Moses, that of the foundation of the monarchy by Saul and David, or that of the Prophets; the classical text, either the Mosaic code, the writings of the Prophets, or the Talmud. For the devotee of the Greco-Roman tradition, the classical age may be either fifth-century Greece, republican Rome, or the period in which the "five good emperors" ruled over the Empire; the classical texts, either Greek or Latin works or some combination of the two. The important point is that a tradition can be defined by the set of texts taken to be in some sense "sacred," as containing models of artistic and intellectual expression and as providing the ideals against which both thought and action can be judged. The classics of a tradition provide the ground for its articulation. No classics, no tradition; no tradition, no classics.

It is necessary to understand the relation between a tradition and its classics in order to understand the role played by *humanism* in Greco-Roman civilization. For humanism is only one strain of that civilization—the most important to many later scholars and intellectuals, but not always the most important or most authoritative to the Greeks and Romans themselves. By humanism we mean an attitude of mind that takes man as the center of the cosmos and then goes on to interpret both the nature of the physical world and significance of the spiritual world in purely human terms. Humanism does not preclude the belief in a spiritual realm or even in the gods or a God. But it does presuppose that man is endowed with the talents and capacities necessary for the establishment of a good life on earth, and it sets human consciousness the task of constructing the bases for such a life out of its own resources.

Of course, there is an ambiguity contained in the very heart of humanistic culture, an ambiguity buried in the notion of "man" himself. For men do not know definitively what "humanity" essentially *is* or what it might ultimately turn out *to be*. "Man" is a problem to men, and humanists are faced with the problem of constructing an adequate human community on earth in the face of contradictory conceptions of their own humanity. This is why the history of any given phase of the humanistic ideal must specify what was the traditional matrix within which that ideal was articulated. Since man is a puzzle to men, any given humanistic ideal must always be articulated within the context of the various antihumanisms present in its environment. This is why, in our account of the humanistic element in Greco-Roman civilization, we have stressed both the religious traditions out of which it developed and the socio-political problems to which it had to address itself. The "humanism" of the Greeks was not the same as that of the Romans; nor could it be, given the differences between their respective religious traditions and the different kinds of social and political problems they faced. And so too for the various "humanisms" of the modern age that pretend to be continuous with the Greco-Roman varieties: Roman Catholic, Greek Orthodox, Protestant, Rationalistic, and Scientific. At the center of each of these humanisms stands a different conception of the nature of man. What makes them all part of the same *tradition* is that they all appeal to Greco-Roman civilization as the *classical* model of their ideal values and use Greek and Roman texts as sources for their own formulations of their specific values.

All this having been understood, we are in a better position to conceptualize the peculiar relation *between* Greeks and Romans *within* the single tradition that we call Greco-Roman. First the Greeks: their humanism, which reached a high point in the fifth century B.C. in Athens, was a sublimated version of their Olympian religion. This religion, highly anthropomorphic, was transformed by the transition from tribal to city life that occurred in the seventh–sixth centuries B.C. The vision of the life of the gods was changed into a vision of what man himself might aspire to by certain thinkers of the century that followed. Perhaps it is inaccurate to speak of the humanization of Greek religion; it might be more proper to speak of a deification of Greek humanity. This process of deification was promoted by Greek success against the Persian Empire, further economic expansion, and the consequent cosmopolitanization of Greek cultural experience.

At the same time, however, the Greeks remained curiously—and fatally—captive of a brand of ethnocentrism that was at once social, cultural, and sexual. The deified humanity that they honored as an ideal was denied in principal to be extendable to slaves, women, most non-Greeks, and (increasingly) even to other Greek males met as enemies in inter-city wars. Greek humanism, then, combined an ideal that was cosmopolitan in principle with a cultural vision that was grossly parochial, not to say barbarous, in practice. The tension between the scope envisioned by the principle and the range envisaged by the practice was perceived by the greatest writers and thinkers of classical Greece; and the analysis of the implications of this tension can be said to stand at the heart of Greek philosophy, literature, historiography, and art alike. It was this tension that frustrated Greek attempts to construct an enduring political unity; and it was this tension that resulted in those conflicts that made Alexander the Great appear as a savior when he descended on Greece to unify it under an oriental despotism.

Alexander represented an effort to provide the cosmopolitan political framework necessary for the implementation of the Greek humanistic ideal. But the effect of his rule was to discourage belief in the possibility of a genuinely humanistic politics. The so-called "Hellenistic" period that he inaugurated in the eastern Mediterranean world did witness a fusion of Greek with Near Eastern, and specifically Persian, cultural traditions. But the wars fought by his successors for control of the entire area undermined faith in anything but a divine deliverance from political anarchy. During this period, the humanistic values of the Greeks tended to take two forms: the highly individualistic teachings of such philosophical sects as the Cynics, Sceptics, and Epicureans; and the highly elitist, and authoritarian, doctrines of the Platonists, Aristotelians, and Stoics. At the same time, the crucial ingredient of Greek humanism, its belief in the powers of reason to solve all specifically human problems, was diluted by the infusion of highly mystical and irrationalist ideas promoted by the religions of the Orient.

It is within a context such as this that the Roman conquest of the Mediterranean world, completed for the most part by the end of the first century B.C., can be understood. The Romans, whatever else they may have been, were the carriers of a political vision that was inherently cosmopolitan and integrating, rather than provincial and divisive, in its main thrust. This is not to suggest that the

Romans were possessed of some mysterious political wisdom that gave to them a foresight lacking to the Greeks, only that their own religious traditions and socio-political experience had prepared them to meet the problems of political unification in the ancient world in a unique way.

The Romans were the custodians of a tradition quite different from that of the Greeks when they entered the course of world history during the third century B.C. They were more archaic, more conservative, and correspondingly more religious than their Greek counterparts. And their religiosity appears to have been of a *kind* quite different from that of the Greeks. Their religion was more intimate, more spiritual, and in the end more communal than either the Olympian or the Orphic varieties of the Greek religious endowment. The brand of humanism that they fostered subsequently was, as a result, more socially constructive, less individualizing, and less atomizing than that of the Greeks.

But the Greeks gradually became the "classic" representatives of the ideals honored by the Romans in their articulation of their empire. Greek thought and art were assimilated by the Roman upper classes as images of the ideals that they aspired to. The Romans' attitude toward Greece was not unlike that of many wealthy Americans toward France in the late nineteenth and early twentieth centuries: Greece for the Romans was the home of true "civilization" and the Greek language was often spoken by the Roman upper classes in preference to their own native Latin. The Romans were not, however, uncritical idolators of their Greek captives. Greek cultural values had been viewed with suspicion by many of the leaders of the Roman Republic from the beginning. The old Romans had perceived the threat that Greek materialism, individualism, and even

rationalism—the mainstays of the humanist world view—
offered to the Roman sense of piety, discipline, and public
responsibility. As a result, Greek cultural ideals were not
imported into Rome in undiluted form. They were fused
with Roman notions of civic responsibility. The product of
this fusion, Roman civic humanism, became the basis of
public ethics and political reconstruction in Rome's golden
age.

It was once conventional to view the decline and
fall of the Roman Empire as a result first of the importa-
tion of Greek values into Rome (which supposedly made
the virile Romans "effeminate"), then of the triumph of
Christianity (which supposedly made the warlike Romans
"otherworldly"). Interpretations such as these are usually
set forth by self-proclaimed "realists" who, in other circumstances, would never think of imputing such causal
efficacy to anything like "ideals" and "values." As a matter
of fact, there is no evidence that the Romans of the first
century A.D. were any "softer" than their Republican counterparts of the first century B.C. Nor is there any reason to
believe that the Romans of the third century A.D. were more
"spiritual" than their predecessors. The breakup of Greco-
Roman civilization was caused—like the breakup of any
civilization—by the inability of Greeks, Romans, and Christians alike to find an adequate solution to certain practical
problems within the limits set for them by the Greco-
Roman "tradition" of thought and action. What happened
in the fourth century A.D. is that people throughout the
Mediterranean world lost confidence, on a grand scale, in
the principal elements of the Greco-Roman world-view.
And many of them went over to Christianity, which seemed
to provide an alternative way of facing reality and even of
transforming it in ways that Greco-Roman humanism could
not even conceive.

There is a danger in using such metaphorical expressions as "rise and fall" or "dissolution" when referring
to the last phase of a civilization's development. Such
metaphors are too materialistic, too reifying of what is
after all more a mode of existence rather than a fixed object.
"Civilizations" like "traditions" are complexes of mental
sets and modes of comportment characteristic of the people
who make them up. When a civilization "dies," it does not
resemble the death of an animal or human being or the
falling apart of a machine. For when civilizations die, the
people who had once sustained them go on living. The
institutional and cultural continuity may be broken, but the
generational series continues. The "death" of Greco-Roman
civilization represented nothing more than the abandonment
of its component "traditions" by people who no longer found
them compatible with the exigencies of life as it had to be
lived in the fourth and fifth centuries A.D. In becoming
"Christian" and "barbarian," these peoples substituted
another set of traditions for those that had sustained the
Greeks and Romans for better than a thousand years. The
Greco-Roman tradition itself did not die. It was merely
consigned to history, to await revival and restoration as a
model of civilized comportment when the Christian and
barbarian traditions began to show their debilities in later
times.

The history of the Western Middle Ages can be
viewed legitimately as a series of renascences, or rebirths,
of culture in which the Greco-Roman tradition played a
progressively more central role as model and guide to
civilized comportment. The Carolingian Renaissance of the
eighth century, the anti-Romanesque Renaissance of the
twelfth century, the Humanist Renaissance of fifteenth-
century Italy, the French Classicism of the seventeenth
century, and the Enlightenment of the eighteenth century

were all, to a certain extent, dependent upon the Greco-Roman tradition for their vitality and influence. The fact that each of these renascences found in the Greco-Roman past a different image of the ideals that had made Greece so brilliant and Rome so enduring should not obscure the importance which those ideals had in giving to Western civilization a unitary course of development. Every one of these revivals was characterized by a rediscovery of the humanistic kernel of the original "classical" age. The Oedipus of Sophocles is not the Oedipus—owner of the famous "complex"—of Sigmund Freud. But what Sophocles and Freud have in common is the search for that essential humanity of which Oedipus was to both a symbol.

H. V. W.

CHRONOLOGY

	GREECE	ROME
B.C. 3000	Appearance of higher civilization in Crete	
1400	Destruction of Knossos	
1230	Sack of Troy	
1200	Movement of the "sea peoples" throughout eastern Mediterranean	
1130	Destruction of Mycenae	
1100	Dorian invasions of Hellas	
1000		Latins settle in Central Italy
750–700	Composition of *Iliad* and *Odyssey*	
700	Hesiod's *Works and Days*	
700–		Etruscan conquest of Southern Italy
621	Draco's legal reforms in Athens	
594	Solon's legal reforms in Athens	
561–527	Pisistratus, tyrant of Athens	
509		Expulsion of Etruscan kings from Rome; foundation of the Roman Republic
508	Cleisthenes' reforms in Athens	
494–479	Persian Wars	
490	Battle of Marathon	
480	Battle of Salamis	
479	Battles of Plataea and Mycale	

B.C.		
478–454	Delian League	
458–431	Age of Pericles in Athens	
451–450		Law of the Twelve Tables
431–404	Peloponnesian Wars	
387		Rome sacked by the Celts
338	Battle of Chaironea; Philip II of Macedon (359–336) conquers Greece	
336–323	Rule of Alexander the Great	
334	Alexander invades the Persian Empire	
331	Foundation of city of Alexander	
326	Alexander's campaigns in Northern India	
323–276	Alexander's successors (Antigonids, Seleucids, and Ptolemies) contend for his empire	
321		Samnites defeat a Roman army at Caudine Forks
304		Samnites defeated by Rome
275		Roman dominance of Italy
264–241		First Punic War; Sicily incorporated into Roman empire
218–201		Second Punic War
216		Battle of Cannae; Hannibal defeats the Romans
215–205	First Macedonian War	
202		Battle of Zama; defeat of Hannibal by Scipio Africanus
149–146		Third Punic War; destruction of Carthage
146	Macedonia and Greece fall to Rome	
135		Slave rebellions in Sicily
133		Assassination of Tiberius Gracchus
121		Assassination of Gaius Gracchus

CLASSICAL GREECE

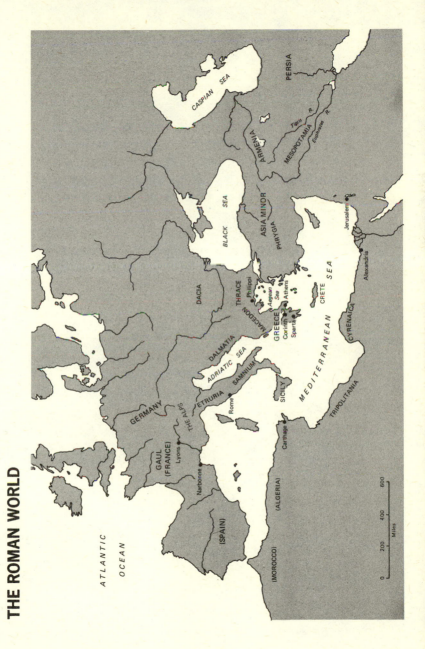

THE ROMAN WORLD

THE
GRECO-ROMAN
TRADITION

THE ESSENCE OF CLASSICISM

The term *Classical Civilization* is conventionally used to characterize a host of cultural traditions that flowed together, fused, and took on a distinctive form in the Mediterranean basin between about 1500 B.C. and A.D. 500. This civilization comprised Greek and Cretan elements, which developed in the northeastern sector of the Mediterranean, Roman elements, which developed in the western part, and various oriental strains, which originated in the Fertile Crescent (Mesopotamia, Syria-Palestine, and Egypt) but had spread over the entire Mediterranean world by the fifth century B.C. We think of this amalgam as Greco-Roman because we are directly affiliated with it in the stage during which the Greeks and Romans put their distinctive stamp on it. But this term should not obscure the fact that many of the institutions, ideas, and art forms that the Greeks and Romans claimed as their own creations were not original with them. Though both tended to look down on peoples who differed from them in language and customs and called such peoples "barbarians," both borrowed widely from their neighbors, friends and foes alike. We do not denigrate the originality of either the Greeks or the Romans by admitting that both built upon the achievements of peoples much older than themselves. In fact, their achievement is understandable only as a continuation of many of those older strains.

But the Greeks and the Romans differed from all other ancient peoples and resembled each other in the tenacity with which they pursued one purpose: the construction of a civilization based on humanistic ideals. Humanism is an attitude of mind that places man at the center of the world-picture and defines humanity's purpose as the creation of a culture dedicated to serving the needs, interests,

1

and aspirations of man alone. The humanistic attitude was not the only one present in Greek and Roman civilization, and in the end it did not even predominate. Nowhere in the ancient world, however, was that attitude taken as seriously as it was in Greece and Rome. Insofar as we honor classical civilization as a still living force today, we honor it for its humanism. Humanism was a difficult ideal to arrive at in the ancient world and even more difficult to realize, but for awhile the Greeks and Romans realized it for a significant part of the ancient Mediterranean area. In that achievement they provided a model for the humanistically oriented culture of the modern age.

Most other ancient peoples were dominated by the belief that the world had been created by forces much more powerful than man, and that man himself had been created to serve those forces. In Mesopotamia and Egypt, the oldest centers of civilized life, culture was organized in such a way as to make man only a secondary beneficiary of the products of his own labor and inventiveness. Throughout the ancient Near East, the state, the social order, the economy, and the customs of everyday life were so ordered as to keep men's attention centered upon their obligations to these "spiritual" figments of their own imaginations. But in Greece during the fifth century B.C. and Rome during the first century B.C., human energies were systematically channeled into the building of a world for men alone.

The Greeks formulated the ideals of this program, and the Romans implemented it for a large portion of humanity. Why they were compelled to attempt this, as well as how, is told briefly in what follows. The ultimate sources of their inspiration are obscure, and will probably never be disclosed to the historian, but the magnificence of their achievement is present for all to see in the remains of Greco-

Roman civilization, preserved in literary, artistic, and architectural monuments, which, let us hope, time will never completely efface.

There is something almost "sinful" about Greco-Roman civilization; an atmosphere of doom seems to hover in the background of its most heroic exertions. In part this is because we view the actions of the Greeks and Romans with the sapient hindsight of the historian; we know how in fact their efforts at human adulation came out. We reconstruct their lives from the *decaying* remains of their activities, which are still present for us. And there is nothing more melancholy than a ruin; it bespeaks the frailty of all things human and forces upon us the realization that nothing escapes the relentless power of time. We are inclined therefore to be indulgent of classical man's optimism, to tolerate rather than appreciate his willfulness. Until, at least, we realize how hard won that optimism was.

The Greeks and the Romans were aware of the dangers involved in their attempts to place man at the center of the world, and they examined the perils of self-pride with surpassing subtlety and insight. They recognized that men run a risk in trying to build a stable world for themselves, that it is easier to take life as it is given by one's ancestors than to try to change it, and that every two steps forward must be paid for by at least one step backward. Yet they found the courage to believe that the game of life was worth the human candle that had to be consumed in the playing of it. And this tragic second sight they regarded as sufficient reward for the difficulties met with in contest with the gods. The tragic vision is probably the most precious legacy of this contest that they have left us.

But the tragic vision was not their only legacy. They also made the first systematic analysis of the operations of human reason, the "pure reason" of Greek philosophy on the one hand and the "practical reason" of Roman political life on the other. Although neither the Greeks nor the Romans attained to the respect for reason that characterizes the modern scientific view of the world, both peoples believed that there was some quantum of reason in the world-process, that the human mind could discern its operations, and that humanity could adapt to, if not control, nature insofar as nature itself was rational. Many Greeks and Romans were convinced that the world was "irrational" only in the extent to which men were ignorant of it. That is to say, they were able to rise above the notion that nature was only a dark arcanum of disorderly forces intent upon the destruction or subjugation of man. At worst, they were inclined to believe, the world was indifferent to man; at best it was both knowable to him and a suitable place for human habitation. Irrationality they also regarded as a human attribute and interpreted it, like evil itself, as a result of human ignorance.

Thus they were driven to a relentless examination of the world in all its immediate variety and ultimate unity. Their thought and art vacillate between the consideration of the various and an apprehension of the unified; they never really succeeded in reconciling these two aspects in which the world offered itself to human consciousness for reflection. But again, in their more lucid moments, they concluded that whatever the ultimate nature of the world, it was generally adequate for the satisfaction of human needs. Abandoning the hope of eternal life or supreme happiness, they contented themselves with a *better* human life, a *provisional* happiness, and a good name in the memories of the men who would come after them.

This interest in the good opinion of future men drove

the Greeks and Romans to an examination of peoples who had preceded them. The Greeks produced the first examples of genuine historical scholarship. Their attempt to resurrect the past in the present was carried forward in Roman times. Because they did not think that the gods were particularly interested in the well-being of men, the Greeks and Romans conceived of a *human* community that stretched across time itself, a community that included men of the past as well as men of the present and future.

History is the humanistic discipline *par excellence*. The historian, unlike the theologian, abandons the attempt to make contact with the gods and contents himself with communication with other men, in other times and places. He is concerned to determine the extent to which all men participate in a common humanity and how they expressed that humanity in different ways. Nothing is more expressive of the humanism of Greco-Roman thought than its historical orientation. Nothing seems more timelessly relevant than the works produced by the great Greek historians Herodotus and Thucydides and their Roman successors Julius Caesar, Suetonius, Livy, and Tacitus. It is not surprising, therefore, that we are inclined to regard the historical works produced by the Greco-Roman world as the nearest thing to a modern social science created by it.

But Greeks and Romans probably would not have shared this view. For them, the humanistic science *par excellence* was not history but rhetoric, the art of eloquence.

We are inclined to think of rhetoric as simply the art of persuasive speaking, as the technique of verbal embellishment, and to set it over against logic—to be used to score points against an opponent in a debate when we do not have the evidence necessary for an adequate case. It is true that during the course of Greco-Roman civilization, rhetoric tended to degenerate into mere "oratory," the sophistic art of making the worse case the better, or the better the worse. But in general the ancients held the art of speaking in much higher esteem than most modern notions of oratory might possibly suggest. Since Greeks and Romans believed that man differed from the other animals primarily by his ability to speak, they also tended to believe that speech was the very basis of whatever "civilization" man could claim. And so the Greeks and Romans carried out, under the study of rhetoric, the first systematic inquiry into the nature of language and communication in general.

This inquiry into language and communication was an earnest of their humanism. For whereas the priests of the archaic civilizations of the Near East may well have been interested in the problem of communication, their primary interest had been in communication with the gods—through prayers and the reading of portents, auguries, and the like. To be sure, among the Greeks and Romans this kind of divination continued to be practiced. We must never forget that throughout the history of the ancient world the greater part of the Greek and Roman populace remained hopelessly bound up in the practices of magic, myth, and superstitious beliefs of the most archaic kind. But in the study of rhetoric, the science of communication among men, the Greeks and Romans turned also to the systematic study of the psychological bases of human community. In inquiring into the problem, How is communication possible? the ancient classical humanists turned also to the problem of how human community is possible. They thereby laid the foundations of those disciplines that we today call the social sciences—psychology, sociology, political economy, anthropology, and so on.

The historical sense and concern with the problem of

communication lay at the base of Greek and Roman thought about law. Whereas the other peoples of the ancient world tended to believe that all law was divine, communicated to men from the gods, the Greeks and Romans worked towards the distinctions between divine, human, and natural law. As a matter of fact, it was the Greeks who first articulated the notion that human law, law made by men, might serve as a protection for men against both nature and the gods. More important, however, was the Greek notion that men were themselves responsible for the creation of the conditions under which they could realistically expect any justice from one another. The Greeks were the first to articulate the ideal of a purely human brand of justice for all citizens within the confines of the city-state. But the Romans were the first to extend this notion to include other peoples as well, to make the ideal of human justice the principle of an international polity. The combination of equity and cosmopolitanism characteristic of Roman law has remained an important ideal in the legal traditions of the West ever since.

In what follows I have concentrated on culture—formal thought, literature, art, historiography, and rhetoric—rather than on politics. For it is the *ideals* of Greco-Roman civilization, rather than its realities, that must interest us as students of our own past seeking orientation in a distressed present. Professor Arnold J. Toynbee has suggested that a great part of the strife of our age has been caused by modern man's promotion of "man worship," which arose first in the "humanism" of the Greeks; and he has counseled that we can find relief from the peculiarly modern forms of suffering only by taking refuge in religion once more. Whether this view is correct or not we cannot say. But such a view is not consistent with the principles that must guide historical thinking in its efforts to make sense of the present by reflection on its relation to various parts of the past. We may agree with Professor Toynbee that if we are to survive, we can do so only by nourishing our capacities for commitment to "ideals" rather than to what appear to be the ineluctable "realities" of our own time. To be sure, the ideals of a past age are not transmissible in their integrity to any future age as a living guide to the men of that age. But the story of how men frame ideals, articulate them, and hold fast to them in adversity is an education in a uniquely human power, the power that distinguishes man from other animals.

We can learn something from another rehearsal of the story of how the Greeks and Romans pursued their ideals. And we may learn something about the dangers of superannuated idealism from reflection on their ultimate fates. The Greeks and Romans, like all peoples, were unable to relinquish those values and institutions that had been outgrown by the times. There is a moral to be found in the study of the refusal by both Greeks and Romans to undertake a fundamental reassessment of their own cultural presuppositions in the face of one failure after another. Perhaps in the contemplation of the results of their obstinacy we may also learn a valuable lesson about ourselves.

GREECE

The Land, the People, and the Inherited Cultural Traditions

THE GEOGRAPHY OF GREECE

The form of a civilization is determined in large part by the physical environment in which it develops. This was especially true of ancient civilizations; their rudimentary technologies allowed only partial and always insecure control over nature and its processes. In ancient times, more so than today, the land set the problems that a people had to solve if it were to survive at all, and nature set the limit on the resources out of which men had to fashion the necessities, both material and spiritual, of civilized existence. Thus, in order to understand the principles underlying Greek civilization, one must know something about the physical environment in which and against which it evolved.

The Greek peninsula, called Hellas by the Greeks, is an extension of the Balkan Mountains. It has always been a hard land; it offered only modest material resources to the settlers who found their way there in prehistoric times. In ancient as in modern times, Greece was frequently

shaken by earthquakes. The instability of the earth therefore belied the apparent friendliness of its brilliant sun and
its crystalline skies. This unstable land was covered by
rocky hills and mountains. Scarcely 20 percent of the land
was suitable for farming, although certain plains—in Thessaly, Attica, and Laconia—were rich and productive by
ancient standards of fertility. Within the peninsula, communication between the valleys and plains was made difficult by mountain ranges whose passes were sometimes
snowbound in the winter and by rivers that were for the
most part unnavigable the year round, dry or torrential
according to season. Thus, although the first settlers of
Greece could live off mixed farming (agriculture and animal husbandry), it was necessary for them to find another
means of subsistence if they were to raise themselves above
savagery. They found another means in the sea.

Compared with the Greek land, the Aegean Sea,
which lies between Greece and Asia Minor (Turkey), must
have seemed positively inviting to ancient men. The coastline of Greece is more than 2500 miles long, marked by in-
lets, coves, and harbors so intrusive that no point on the
Greek mainland lies more than forty miles from sea water.
The absence of tides in the Mediterranean encouraged navi-
gation between the coastal towns and villages, and although
northern winds often whipped the sea to fury and imperiled
the lives of those who ventured too far from shore, the
distances between the many islands that dot the Aegean
were short and could be covered relatively easily even in
ancient ships. Boats ran between the islands towards Asia
Minor, Cyprus, and Crete when the wind was fair and took
refuge in sheltered coves when the sea grew angry. The
Greeks therefore turned to the sea for sustenance as naturally as the men of the Fertile Crescent turned to the

soil. Instead of directing all their energies inward to the conquest of neighboring valleys and plains, the Greeks slid off the sloping hills of their native gulfs into the warm, clear waters of the Mediterranean to augment their gleanings from the land by seafaring, first as fishermen and pirates, then as traders, and finally as rulers of extensive maritime empires. This investment in the sea gave an added dimension to Greek economic life. In many respects, Greek civilization as we know and honor it was a gift of the sea. Greek history is the story of a succession of cultures that exploited that gift in different ways, and the triumphs as well as the tragedies of Greek civilization are ultimately linked to the opportunities presented by a geographical environment in which the sea appeared less a barrier to expansion than a means of communicating with distant horizons.

THE FORMATION OF THE GREEK PEOPLE

Little is known about the people who inhabited the land from earliest times. Presumably, they lived in a condition of typical neolithic savagery. They were settled in small villages, were organized in clans or tribes, scratched their existence from the land, worshiped fertility deities, practiced magic, and shaped their tools and weapons out of stone. To the original inhabitants were added ethnic and cultural stocks brought in by migrations of two groups of peoples from abroad. One group, from Asia Minor or Syria, occupied southern Thessaly; another, whose precise origin is unknown but which possibly originated in the Danube valley to the north, settled in Macedonia and northern Thessaly. These invaders merged with the native population and raised the culture of the area from savagery to barbarism by the introduction of more advanced techniques of farming and animal husbandry, the use of metals, and more complex social institutions, thereby creating the bases for a more stable social life. The process of ethnic fusion was complete by about 1900 B.C., and no further incursions disturbed the style of life thus established until around 1150 B.C., when fresh invasions from the north strengthened the ethnic and cultural elements that had originated in the Danubian plain. From the latter date on, we may properly designate the inhabitants of the Greek mainland as Hellenes, or Greeks, for as they moved southward from Thessaly into Attica and the Peloponnese, they brought with them the characteristic dialects that provided the basis of what we recognize as the Greek language.

MINOAN CIVILIZATION

Higher civilization, however, first appeared in the Aegean basin not on the Greek mainland, but to the south, on the island of Crete. Migrants whose origin is unknown but who were familiar with the advanced agricultural life developed in the Fertile Crescent in the fourth millennium B.C. had settled the islands of Crete, Cyprus, and the Cyclades by about 3000 B.C. The people that settled in Crete are called Minoan after the legendary king Minos, who is supposed to have united the island under a single dynasty at one time. The Minoans quickly applied advanced technical skills to agriculture, seafaring, manufacturing, and trade and created a civilization almost as rich and sophisticated—though not as enduring—as those that appeared in Mesopotamia and Egypt at about the same time.

During the second millennium B.C., the Minoans traded with the barbarian mainland of Greece and the richer centers of civilization in Egypt and Syria. By around 2000 B.C. they had created an autonomous sphere of economic activity. The appearance of rich cities such as Knossos on the northern coast of Crete attests to the growing importance of Minoan trade with the barbarian Greeks who were then settling around the Aegean basin. By 1700 B.C. the Minoans had developed a more efficient written language for the maintenance of records and communication within the vast commercial empire thus created. They abandoned the pictographic form of writing that they had originally used and created a linear script, which we call Linear A, comprising a syllabary without vowels. The Minoans' control of the sea allowed them the luxury of living in great cities that stood open to the water and gave them that security without which higher civilization is impossible.

What is most striking about the Minoans is the apparently secondary role that religious worship and ritual played in their *public* life. That the Minoans were religious is undeniable. But they seem to have been neither fearful of their gods nor particularly grateful to them for services rendered in the creation of their particular style of life. Their art, which appears in sculpture, in frescoes decorating the great palaces, and on pottery, depicts the human body with grace, elegance, and a distinct feeling of delight with life equaled in ancient times only by the Egyptians during the Old Kingdom.

Evidence offered by artistic remains suggests that the men and women of this civilization mixed freely in sports and games. In fact, the feminine element seems to have predominated in the Minoan imagination. Scenes of war are rare, and there is little evidence of profound meditation on the fact of death. The Minoans apparently did not worship their dead, as did most other peoples of the time, out of fear of departed spirits or in hope that the dead would aid them in living their lives on earth; this suggests that they contemplated the afterlife without either anxiety or optimism. They seem to have channeled their energies all but exclusively into the exploitation of the material opportunities offered by their favored position at the center of eastern Mediterranean trading routes, their advanced technology, and the pleasures offered by their wealth and security.

It has been suggested that the secular character of Minoan culture was inspired by the apparent ineffectiveness of fertility gods brought from their original homeland to the barren soil of Crete. The absence of great temples and the presence of small personal shrines in individual homes may bespeak a certain lack of interest in the gods. Perhaps after their arrival in Crete, the Minoans' gods ceased to produce the sustenance for the people in their usual way and were, as a result, relegated to the hearth and household, to serve as protectors of the fertility, wealth, and power of the family alone. This conclusion is supported by the plans of Minoan cities, which, unlike their counterparts in the Fertile Crescent, seem to be laid out, not according to some liturgical specification, symmetrically in relation to the cardinal points of the imagined cosmos or with reference to a great central temple, but randomly and asymmetrically, as though they had grown by chance and in response to primarily practical needs. In any event, if the later Greeks, who borrowed from this civilization, required a precedent for their attempt to build a culture dedicated to the enjoyment of the earthly life, they possessed such a precedent in their ancestors, the Minoans.

The fusion of Cretan civilization and the Greek culture of the mainland began sometime after 2000 B.C., with influences working from south to north originally, as Minoan trade and political relations with the barbaric mainland increased. But influences soon began to move in the other direction. Traces of the mainland culture appear most dramatically in the Cretan city of Knossos between 1450 and 1400 B.C. Here we find a new linear script, definitely Greek in origin, called Linear B and only recently deciphered, which remained in use until around 1200 B.C. Other evidences of mainland influence are manifested in the art, technology, and increasingly warlike tone of the life of the city.

The reasons for the changes in the life of Knossos are not known. Perhaps the city was seized by a Mycenaean raiding party. In any event, the transformation of Knossos marked the beginning of the end for the Cretans. Around 1400 B.C. Knossos was sacked and burned to the ground. A similar fate befell most of the other major Cretan cities shortly thereafter. It was long believed that the destruction of the Cretan cities was the work of northern marauders who had grown tired of being exploited by their richer but more effete neighbors to the south. Some scholars now think that the fall of Crete was caused by an alliance of piratical powers in the eastern Mediterranean, located on Cyprus perhaps, who were desirous of breaking the Cretan monopoly of trade with the northern Aegean. Still others incline to the view that the cities were destroyed by earthquakes and tidal waves.

In any event, Crete never recovered its former position. Although it remained an important center of wealth and culture in the Aegean, exercising considerable civilizing influence on the cruder peoples of the Greek main-

land, especially in the Peloponnese, for another three centuries, military power now shifted definitively to the north,
where a new culture—called Mycenaean—had taken shape.

MYCENAEAN CULTURE

By around 1450 B.C. a semicivilized culture, the Mycenaean, influenced by Minoan civilization but dominated by
an interest in war rather than trade, in expansion by force
rather than commerce, had taken shape in the northern
Peloponnese. Two centuries later, this culture had spread
its influence over most of the Greek mainland, owing largely
to its mastery of a new technology. New building techniques
allowed the Mycenaeans to construct great fortified strong-
holds, while new forms of military organization gave them
a decisive advantage over their foes in Asia Minor and
Crete.

The Mycenaeans worshiped deities connected with
the sky, thunder, and the mountains—the gods of war and
blood—rather than the dove, the snake, and the bull, sym-
bolic of the creative forces of the earth, which were venerated by their more peaceful neighbors. It is true that the
Mycenaeans did not depend upon war alone to sustain them.
A subject peasantry worked the land for them, and they
learned the advantages of trade from the Minoans. But they
preferred to fight and often banded together in great ex-
peditions, such as the one that sacked Troy in the thirteenth
century B.C. and provided the subject for Homer's *Iliad*.
They might have undergone a normal evolution to higher
civilization had the martial element in their culture not
been strengthened by the necessity of withstanding invaders
from the north and west, who infiltrated the eastern Medi-

terranean in the late thirteenth century B.C. Gradually the great Mycenaean feudal baronies broke up into smaller fighting bands, each dedicated to the destruction of all the others and all contributing to the weakening of the whole. The result was that when, in the twelfth to eleventh centuries B.C., a barbarian people from the Balkans, the Dorians, found their way into Greece, they were able to move virtually unopposed all the way to Crete, sacking and pillaging wherever they went.

The Dorians spoke a Greek dialect and could ultimately be assimilated, but not before they had effected the last major reshuffling of the Greek ethnic map. Bypassing Attica, the Dorians moved down into the Peloponnese, where they formed the basis of the later Spartan population of Laconia. They then pushed out onto the islands of the Aegean and the western coast of Asia Minor. Evidences of their impact are discernible as far as Cyprus in the south. They dealt the death blow to Cretan culture and hurled the Greek world into an age of chaos as dark as that of the early Middle Ages in Europe.

From the eleventh to the eighth centuries B.C., literate civilization virtually disappeared in the Aegean. When it finally reappeared in the seventh century, it was centered, not on the Greek mainland, but in Asia Minor, in Ionia, where the Greeks had come into contact with the city-dwelling peoples of the Mesopotamian cultural bloc. Here the unique elements of Greek culture as we know it made their first appearance. What we recognize as Greek literature, Greek science and philosophy, and Greek political institutions took shape in cities such as Chios, Samos, and Miletus in Ionia. From there they were exported to the Greek mainland—to flourish in the sixth century in cities such as Athens, Thebes, and Corinth.

THE WORLD OF HOMER

Our knowledge of this world of Ionia and of the cast of mind that characterized its people is provided by the closest thing to the Hebrew Bible ever produced in Greece, the epic poems of Homer. Homer was supposedly a blind bard who flourished in Ionia, possibly in the city of Chios, possibly during the eighth century B.C.; at least, the poems attributed to him were probably given the form in which they have been transmitted to us in that area at about that time. Some scholars believe that Homer's poems were the product of at least two poets writing in different areas at different times. This is because the *Iliad* deals with the siege of Troy, which occurred in the thirteenth or twelfth century, whereas the *Odyssey*, the story of Odysseus's wanderings during his return to his homeland after the fall of Troy, describes a social world that could have existed only as late as the eighth century. The *Iliad* describes the manners and ideals of a class of nobles dedicated to the art of war as a way of life and stresses almost exclusively the martial virtues of the hero; while the *Odyssey* describes a settled, agricultural people possessing an advanced technology, gentler manners, and a respect for intellectual virtues that may have appeared only later in Greek history. No doubt Homer was a transmitter of an oral tradition that had descended to him from the remote past, just as the earliest parts of the Bible had descended to the Israelites; but Homer, like the Hebrew editors of the Bible, gave a unitary form and style of expression to the tradition. Whatever the differences in moral outlook and references to everyday life that distinguish superficially the *Iliad* from the *Odyssey*, there are enough similarities between them to justify regarding them as the creation of a single genius.

The Greeks themselves entertained no serious doubts as to Homer's authorship of both works even while recognizing fully that he was providing them with a synthesis of the various cultural traditions that differentiated them from all other peoples. We may therefore linger with profit on Homer's work in order to understand what it was that the Greeks themselves valued in their own past and how it was that they were able to build upon it a civilization devoted principally to man.

Above all, the Greeks found in Homer a catalogue of models on which to construct a vision of the heroic life. In the *Iliad* the ideals of the old aristocratic society are represented quintessentially by the hero Achilles, the greatest of the Greek warriors. Achilles is the prototype of the tragic hero who labors under a fate that forces him to choose either a short, arduous life of achievement and fame or a long, serene, but quite undistinguished existence as an ordinary man. Achilles' decision to live the life of a hero and to attain glory was justified by the fame he enjoyed among later men. Since there is no description of the afterlife in the *Iliad*, the present life appears as the place within which whatever happiness a man can aspire to must be achieved. The only immortality vouchsafed to man is the good name accorded him by his friends and descendants. The only standard for determining whether one has had a good life or not is the feeling on the part of the individual, confirmed by the fame he enjoys, that he has fully realized the potential for heroic action given him by fate at his birth.

The virtue of an individual can be envisaged as the nucleus of creative energy present within him; this nucleus of energy also sets limits on what he is capable of doing during his lifetime. The problem of life, according to the Homeric vision, is to release this energic fund before one is called to sink once more into the indifferent universe, which is the source of everyone and everything. Only the man who courageously embraces his fate has a chance of happiness. The coward who refuses to take up the contest and chooses prudence over aspiration may live to a ripe old age, but he is fit only for the work of women and slaves and has no place in the councils of heroes.

Of course, Achilles is a rather limited type of hero. His excellence manifests itself in his physical attributes, his speed, strength, and courage. He is not introspective, and he confronts the world around him primarily as a stage upon which to display his virtues as an athlete, warrior, and rival of the gods in physical beauty. Odysseus represents a more advanced stage of cultural growth insofar as his virtues include those of the intellectual hero. Odysseus is not only strong, handsome, and courageous, he is also, and above all, cunning, reflective, eloquent, and sensitive to psychological nuances in those around him. He sees the world less as a stage than as an enemy, which he must resist and overcome by powers that are specifically human rather than generally animal. He was much more the complete man, which Greek culture was to take as an ideal in later centuries, than was Achilles.

The land to which Odysseus seeks to return—Ithaca —is a happy land, alive with fields, flocks, and vineyards. It was still shot through with potential violence (as the demeanor of Penelope's suitors shows), but on the whole it was an orderly land—inviting, restful, and secure. In Ithaca a warrior could rest from the trials of battle, surrounded by his sons and retainers, content to test his virtue in contest with the soil for its riches and bounty. Thus, taken together, the *Iliad* and the *Odyssey* represent a spectrum of the kinds of virtue that might be found in a man. They also represent a catalogue of the kinds of situations that the ancient Greeks thought a man might encounter during the course of his life. The works are epics in that they show the hero turning these situations into occasions for the expression of his powers, both physical and intellectual, from which his fame might be fashioned.

The epic, as a literary genre, has other attributes that can be specified to illuminate the kind of world in which it arises as a dominant literary form. The most important of these attributes is the absence of any significant time dimension or notion of historical development. Much *happens* in the *Iliad*, but very little *develops*. Of course, the *story* of Achilles can be said to develop from the point at which we encounter him, sulking in his tent and refusing to join the Greeks in their effort to take Troy, to the point at which he re-enters the fight, defeats Hector in battle, and prepares the way for the Greek triumph in the end. But the passage of time effects no fundamental *transformations* in either the physical or the moral attributes of the characters involved in the action. Even in the *Odyssey*, Odysseus and Penelope still *look* substantially the same as they are supposed to have done twenty years earlier, when Odysseus departed on the expedition to Troy. The German scholar Erich Auerbach has suggested that, in contrast to the most imposing figures of the Old Testament, such as Abraham, the heroes of the Greek epics lack *interiority*. Everything that happens to them is depicted in terms of an external cause acting upon them, to which they respond; he has suggested that this conception of the exteriority of relationships, which is characteristic of Homer's world-view, is what gives to subsequent Greek thought and literature its peculiarly naturalistic flavor.

To be sure, in the subsequent evolution of Greek sensibility, and especially in Greek tragedy, the conception of the passage of time and the development of interiority in the tragic heroes come to the fore. But this is a late development, the product of the Greek experience of the social world of the city-state, where different classes come into conflict, different conceptions of justice and virtue are possible, and the problem of individual responsibility for actions with unforeseen consequences is forced upon thought.

In Homer's world, art exists for the entertainment and edification of a single class, the warrior aristocracy; the epic, with its suggestion that the ideals of this class are of timeless validity and are therefore unquestionable, must be seen as a natural form for the literary representation of the world to take. In terms of the actions that are actually depicted, there are no crucial distinctions between heroes and gods, between the social and the natural forces at work in the world. These all exist in such a way as to suggest *both* their ideality *and* their concreteness, their eternality *and* their temporality, simultaneously. The great moral conflicts that rack the heroes of the Old Testament, such as King David or King Saul, are not to be found in the world inhabited by Homer's heroes. Types of heroes similar to David and Saul—Prometheus, Oedipus, and Antigone— are produced by Greek writers only much later, in the context of the city-state, which supplants the world of the tribe and its self-conscious egotism as described by Homer.

GREEK RELIGION

The Greeks originally worshiped a pantheon of gods, who were conceived to have powers over the various parts of the cosmos (such as the sky, the sea, and the under-

world), forces (such as wind, thunder, rain), states of affairs (war, peace), or qualities (wisdom, beauty, strength).
The conventional number of deities was twelve. These gods
had their home on Mount Olympus, the highest peak in
Greece, and they were supposed to be ruled over by a kind
of constitutional monarch, Zeus, and his queen, Hera. Pe-
riodically, the gods abandoned their care of cosmic functions and their contests with each other and intervened directly in human affairs. In all their activities the gods
were conceived to be motivated by the same interests, passions, and desires that motivated men. They possessed the
same virtues and vices as men and lived a kind of superior
version of human life. With one important difference, however: whereas human beings were mortal, the gods were
immortal. They did not have to face the prospect of death,
and so, as the Greeks imagined them, they entered into all
their projects with a daring, a gaiety, and a kind of in-
souciance that even the most heroic of mortal men might
not inspire to. In short, they lived life as men might live it
if they possessed the courage, beauty, and wisdom of the
hero and were liberated from the nagging realization that
someday they must die.

This religion was quintessentially anthropomorphic,
then, and even humanistic, since the life of the god was
merely the life of man raised to a higher power. The philosopher Nietzsche says of this ancient Greek religion that
it was the most humanly ennobling religion ever conceived:
for the Greek gods justified human life by living it to the
full for all eternity.

But the gods' power was not unlimited. Though the
gods were immortal, they were not eternal. They had been
created at a particular point in time, and they were limited
by the fact that the world-process that had given birth to

them was immutable, fixed in its essence—and the basic nature of the world-process not even the gods could challenge.

This led to the belief that the gods were primarily a kind of executive branch of a system of cosmic government greater than themselves. The informing principle of this cosmic government the Greeks called fate (*moira*). Fate was the actual order of the world, and not even the gods could challenge fate with impunity.

Each of the gods had been consigned a particular part of the cosmos to administer. A particular god, such as the sea-god Poseidon, might tinker with tides or cause an earthquake, but he could not do anything he pleased with the water and the earth; there were limits to what he could do. So too a given god or goddess might intervene in a military campaign and forestall its outcome for some time, but if it was fated that a city, like Troy, was to fall, then fall it must in the end, whatever any of the gods desired. When a god transgressed the limits of his authority, he was punished in accordance with the rules of cosmic justice, to which both gods and men were subject.

The gods differed from men in another important respect also. They had greater knowledge of the world-process; they could foretell the future and within their respective provinces even determine it up to a certain point. Thus they did not labor in the ignorance or uncertainty that men did. When they transgressed the limits of their authority, they knew what they were doing, because they enjoyed a perspective on the cosmos denied to man. Therefore, the gods were not heroic in the eyes of the Greeks, for ultimately they ran no radical risk in trying to carry out their plans. But since they enjoyed greater power and knowledge than men, they were called upon by men for guidance, enlightenment, and aid when a new project was being embarked upon, the outcome of which was problematical.

This religion was inevitably unsettling to men and ultimately destructive of confidence in the gods. Since there were some things that not even the gods could do, no man could never be sure that his prayers would be answered, however sympathetic the god might be to the worshiper. And, since the gods had all the vices, as well as the virtues, of men, they were as undependable as men themselves—as fickle, as perverse, as jealous, as any man. Moreover, since there were *many* gods, they might dispose themselves on different sides of a particular issue, and the ire of one might cancel out the goodwill of another, thus leaving the issue as doubtful as before the petition to the god had been entered. Finally, since the gods often intervened in human affairs out of personal motives—love for a human woman, anger at a man, jealousy of the courage or power of a king—the litigant could never be sure that the god to whom he prayed was not already involved in the affair at issue as an interested participant.

All of this undermined the Greeks' confidence in their gods. The Greek might fear his gods, but it was very difficult for him to love them and almost impossible to respect them. As the Greeks gradually succeeded in building purely human defenses of human dignity and needs in the city-states (*poleis*), they tended to turn from the contemplation of the gods to the search for the cosmic principle (fate) which disposed the destinies of both gods and men. If the nature of this mysterious world-principle could be discerned, the Greeks felt, then it might be possible to bypass the gods altogether and achieve a kind of harmony with that world-process—a harmony that would make human life godlike in its order and stability, if not in its longevity and power. It was this attempt to discover the principle by which even the gods were regulated that gave birth to Greek philosophy and science. But the birth of philosophy and science out of the world of mythic religiosity depicted in Homer's epics was not a result of Greek thought and imagination working in a historical void. Philosophy and science were products of new social circumstances, particularly of the circumstances of city living. Before analyzing these new forms of Greek intellectual expression, then, we must first describe the transition from the tribe to the *polis*.

The Political Evolution of Greece

FROM TRIBE TO POLIS

The Greeks about whom Homer writes in the *Iliad* were organized in clans held together by belief in descent from a common ancestor and devotion to a common pantheon of gods. On great cooperative enterprises such as the attack on Troy, the clans formed into larger fighting units (tribes) under the leadership of a war-chief (such as Achilles). The tribes in turn were marshaled under a king, such as Agamemnon, whose authority was always very tenuous and whose power of command waxed and waned with the success or failure of the enterprise. At the end of the expedition, the clans dispersed, each returning to its own territory to devote itself to fighting with neighboring clans, to maintaining control over the slaves and peasants who worked the land, or to intraclan feuding among heads of families.

Within the clan itself the basic unit was the male

head of family, whose power over his wives and children was absolute. The head of the family sacrificed to the ancestral gods and spirits, voted in the clan councils, and represented all members of the family in judicial disputes over property or defended the family's honor by the code of the blood feud. Only the head of family had what we might term a public personality, or rights within the clan. The women and children of the family owed everything to the father, who might dispose of their property and even their lives as he desired.

As can be readily seen, the social system was potentially unstable, for the principal guarantee of justice was individual physical strength or cunning. In enterprises that required large-scale cooperation, the safety of the entire group might be endangered by the whim of a single warrior, such as Achilles who, offended by Agamemnon's confiscation of a captive woman, withdrew from the fight against the Trojans at a critical moment and sulked in his tent with impunity until his offended honor had been satisfied. Members of the clan who lacked the strength of an Achilles were dependent upon their families alone to guarantee security and justice to them. If the family to which the individual belonged was poor or weak, that family could hope for very little of justice or security. So, too, *within* the family. The son or daughter subjected to the rule of a tyrannical father had no recourse; he had to comply with whatever the father demanded of him or leave the family and set out on his own.

This system was adequate for the relatively simple needs of barbarian existence. The continual movement of the tribe, its ceaseless wars, and the variable food supply, which all too often ebbed below the level of subsistence, kept the group at a relatively constant size and allowed only

the strongest to survive. But once the warrior-nomads settled
on the lands of Hellas, became more domesticated, turned to
farming and animal husbandry, and achieved a more stable
social order, the resulting security combined with an increased food supply to cause a radical increase in the population. The increase in the population meant that the holdings of the individual family soon became inadequate to the
needs of all the individuals in it, which led to chronic land-
hunger. Younger sons were unable to support themselves on
inherited lands, and the family, which had once been a
source of security, became increasingly a burden against
which the more adventurous spirits among the Greeks soon
rebelled. The Boeotian poet Hesiod, writing around 700 B.C.,
gave literary expression to the growing dissatisfaction with
the older tribal society, in which might alone made right.
In his *Works and Days*, Hesiod defended the cause of the
peasant who worked the land and earned his bread through
his mastery of the secrets of nature. He deplored the rule
of force, which allowed the warrior to deprive the farmer
of the fruits of his toil, and called for a rule of law that
would lead to an order among men similar to the harmony
the farmer had discovered in nature.

The population explosion of the eighth century B.C.
had a profound effect on Greek social institutions and cultural ideals. Many younger sons left the family to seek their
fortunes elsewhere, as soldiers of fortune and marauders,
as colonists in foreign lands, or as traders and manufac-
turers. The emotional and religious ties that had linked the
individual to the family and the family to the clan were
challenged as unnecessarily restrictive and productive of
strife rather than of security and justice. During this period,
there developed in the cities that grew up on the Greek
mainland a great division between those who worked the

soil and those who derived their livelihood primarily from manufacture and trade. The lyric poets of the seventh and sixth centuries B.C. reflect the resulting social tension, some of them speaking in pessimistic tones of the awful future awaiting a mankind that has lost respect for its traditional gods and values, others lamenting the decline in the status of the warrior, or aristocratic, class.

But there was no turning back to the older ways. In the end, the Greeks abandoned the society based on blood kinship and formed a new society based on the exchange of mutually beneficial social and economic functions. For the older rule of brute force and tradition they substituted codes of written laws designed to assure security for the individual and justice in the group, without appeal to force. In place of the tribe, clan, and family, the Greeks of the sixth century substituted the city-state (*polis*) as the basic social unit. The idea of the city-state was not unique with them, but among the Greeks it was given a unique development, which affected Greek culture definitively and made of the Greek people one of the most explosively creative forces in the ancient world.

THE GREEK CITY-STATE AS IDEAL

The Greek city-state, or *polis* (plural: *poleis*), was unique in the ancient world in that it was conceived primarily as a man-made institution, established by men and for men, to create a realm of order and justice in an otherwise threatening universe. Although each city had a patron god or goddess who was supposed to watch over it in return for sacrifices and ritual worship, the Greek city was not conceived to exist primarily for service to the god (as in Mesopotamia) or as an administrative center within a larger political whole (as in Egypt). The geography of Greece discouraged establishment of a single political center, and the Greeks' conception of the fickleness of the gods made it imprudent for them to vest too much confidence in the gods as guarantors of human well-being. If men were to attain to a stable and secure existence in this world, the Greeks felt, it would be by the agency of men alone. They believed that men, unlike other animals, had been given rational faculties and a capacity to learn from observation of the various social experiments made by different men in different times and places. If a social order within which men could live out their lives with minimal security was to be fashioned, then, it could be done only on the basis of a full and conscious exploitation of purely human capacities.

Another important characteristic of the Greek *polis* was the belief that the *law* that governed it might be the creation of men rather than of gods. If man differed from the animal by virtue of his powers of reasoning, he also differed by his capacity to submit voluntarily to the rule of law. The barbarian, the Greeks believed, was subject to the whims of the passions and instincts; the civilized man was able to control the demands of the passions and to submit himself to the rule of law. Mere existence did not constitute a human life; *humanity* aspired not only to life but to the *good* life, that is, to a life that allowed the development of the highest talents of the individual over and above his immediate animal needs. It was possible to have the good life only by joining with other men in the common effort of providing the minimal needs of security and justice, which meant putting aside certain animal impulses in the interest of the survival of the group. Whereas the tribal society had been made up of willful individuals united by blood and the power of the strongest, the *polis* was to be a society of men linked together in a common effort to realize the good life for all its citizens. The law dictated the terms of membership in this new society and defined the rules for protecting property, disposing power, and administering justice to both the individuals and the classes and groups that made up the city.

In the earliest days of the city's development, when social strife was greatest, the Greeks called upon wise men, or sages, to write a law for them. This recourse to the wise man showed the Greek trust in the power of men to legislate for themselves without the aid of the gods. In Athens a certain Draco, in 621 B.C., provided the first code of Greek law that we know to have been written; it made the trial procedures to be followed in various sorts of cases a matter of public record. Even more important was the legislation of Solon of Athens in 594 B.C. Solon's code seems to have appealed to the ideal of justice for all as the sole basis for a human community and to have envisaged a society in which men with different tasks, skills, and aspirations would be allowed to follow their individual callings in peace and security, as long as they complied with the law.

Since Greek law was conceived as a creation of men and not of the gods, it could in principle be changed by men as necessity required. But a suitable means by which the law could be reformed without resorting to violence was not at first self-evident. The sixth century was a time of social conflict all over Greece. In the course of time, however, most Greeks settled upon oligarchical democracy as the characteristic form of their *poleis*. That is, they vested authority to implement, interpret, and change the law in a body of officials elected by the free and wealthier adult male members of the *polis* and tied the law to the well-being of the group as a whole, *as that body interpreted it.*

While most Greek states were oligarchic, some were democratic. The democratic Greeks, however, regarded the rule of law as tied to the principle of the greatest good for the greatest number *of the citizenry.* On the whole, they were not interested in anyone who did not enjoy citizen status—such as slaves, children, women, and foreigners; and they felt only the vaguest obligation to mankind at large. The *polis*, in short, was essentially egocentric in its outlook, providing security and justice to the ingroup, but to it alone.

On the other hand, most Greeks did not believe that the form of government settled on by any particular *polis* was necessarily better than other forms or that it could be exported for use by people in other places. The form of government and the system of laws were to be dictated by the specific needs of the group framing them and had to be adjusted to the specific environmental pressures, both physical and social, that existed where the group lived. Thus the *polis* might be democratic, oligarchical, aristocratic, or monarchical, as the people it comprised desired. This made for a general political tolerance among the Greeks, but it also promoted a distinct particularism, which made intercity cooperation difficult when a common danger threatened.

With all this in mind, one can see how cities as different in aims and methods of government as Athens and Sparta both qualify as *poleis*. Both cities purported to provide security and justice for their citizens, but each defined its aims and goals differently, and hence required different kinds of laws and different institutions to do its work. Athens, originally a great center of agriculture, manufacture, and trade, became in the fifth century B.C. the administrative center of a great empire. There a relatively open and flexible society took shape, characterized by a broad freedom for its citizens, hospitality for the foreigner who could contribute to the well-being of the city, and a general tolerance for new ideas and institutions. In Sparta, which remained an agricultural center pure and simple, the needs of the citizens were different, and they required a different system of government to provide for those needs.

EFFECT OF URBANIZATION
ON GREEK CULTURE

The organization of the mainland Greeks into cities inaugurated a period of stability, wealth, further population expansion, and social and economic experimentation which made of Greece a great force in the Mediterranean. Greek traders and colonists ranged over the entire Mediterranean basin in the late seventh century B.C., spreading westward to Sicily, southern Italy, France, and Spain; eastward to Asia Minor; southward to North Africa, in the areas not already claimed by the Phoenicians; and northward to the Black Sea. Trade with the colonies allowed many of the cities in Hellas to transform themselves into manufacturing centers or to concentrate on the development of specialized crops such as the grape and the olive, products that could be traded for grain, minerals, and furs with the colonial frontiersmen.

Professor Arnold J. Toynbee has suggested that Greek expansion during this period was made easier by the fact that the great powers of the eastern Mediterranean were temporarily distracted by a contest between Assyria and Persia for control of the entire Fertile Crescent, a contest that had affected Phoenician shipping adversely and had, therefore, led to the decline of Carthage for the moment. When the Persians finally triumphed over Assyria, Toynbee suggests, Greek expansion eastward was halted. At the same time, in the middle of the sixth century, an alliance between Carthage in North Africa and the Etruscans in central Italy cut off the western Greeks from their homeland.

But the original period of intense economic activity and expansion had already caused radical changes in Greek life on the mainland. The population of Greece continued to grow, causing land-hunger, inflation, and depression of the peasantry and those parts of the aristocracy dependent upon the wealth produced by landed holdings, but, at the same time, sudden prosperity for the manufacturer and trader. This situation generated feelings of resentment between the agricultural and commercial sectors of the population, and revolutions soon rocked the Greek city-states. Sparta was not affected by these pressures, but Athens was; her responses to them set the course of her history for the next two hundred years.

Sometime in the eighth century B.C., the Spartans had determined to meet the challenge of land-hunger, not by trade and colonization, like the Athenians, but by expansion at the expense of their neighbors, the Messenians. They conquered the land of Messenia, subjugated the populace, and tied them to the land as serfs (*helots*) of the Spartan state. In order to maintain their control over the *helots*, however, the Spartan citizens had to subject themselves to the harshest kind of political and military discipline. All Spartans were trained for war from the age of seven, and they lived their lives as keepers of an armed citadel in the midst of a hostile and potentially rebellious alien population. In return for the lands they had appropriated from the Messenians, the Spartans had to surrender their own individual liberties. They channeled all of their energies into the maintenance of their state. This gave them an exceptional stability, but it was the stability of the barracks —and as little creative. They did not have to face the pressures the Athenians faced in the sixth century B.C., but neither did they enjoy the period of creativity that those pressures induced in the Athenian populace.

The pressures of class struggle in Athens caused the temporary abrogation of Solon's reforms; for a while full power was exercised by popular leaders from the depressed aristocracy supported by the disgruntled peasantry. Yet in Athens the rule of a number of tyrants—of whom Pisistratus (561–527 B.C.) is an example—did not result in permanent dictatorship. Pisistratus used his popularity with the masses to effect political reforms that ultimately completed the work begun by Solon. Under his leadership Athens was transformed into a limited democracy. Increasingly, power was vested in the economically self-sufficient sectors of the population, but the poorer citizens were not denied a voice in civic affairs. By 508 B.C., his successor Cleisthenes had completed this work of transforming Athens from a chaotic jumble of conflicting factions into an integrated political unit.

Cleisthenes divided Attica into ten local divisions, composed alike of aristocrats, artisans and traders, and peasants. These were used as a basis for voting on all political and military affairs and discouraged the division of the populace along class lines. Next, he founded the Council of the Five Hundred as the chief organ of government. The Council prepared the business of the Popular Assembly in which every citizen had a voice and a vote. He also reformed the courts to guarantee justice to every citizen and to secure to the individual his right of testament, which finally severed the cords that bound the individual to the family. Finally, he placed the army, composed of free citizens rather than of slaves or mercenaries, under the direction of ten generals democratically elected, one from each ward. By the time of Cleisthenes' death, the Athenian government was in good working order. Athens was ready to resume her expansionist policies and to contend with the mighty Persian Empire itself if necessity required.

THE PERSIAN WARS: 494–479 B.C.

The Greeks did not appear to their contemporaries as a puny and inconsequential people upon whom the mighty Persians fell in the hope of an easy victory. By the beginning of the sixth century B.C. the Greek commercial network was potentially as powerful as any other force in the Mediterranean, even if it lacked a single political center or a unified economic purpose. It might even be argued that it was the Greeks who pressed the Persians into war and continued the offensive long after the Persians had sought to withdraw from the contest for control of the Aegean and Black seas. Nor was the Greek offensive limited to the eastern Mediterranean. At about the same time that the Ionian Greeks, supported by mainland cities such as Athens, decided to rebel against their Persian overlords in the east, the western Greeks on Sicily, under the leadership of Syracuse, came into conflict with the Carthaginians and Etruscans. The Greeks appeared to be making their bid for total hegemony in the Mediterranean against the most powerful heirs of the great civilizations of the Fertile Crescent, which had dominated the area for over a thousand years. They almost succeeded in uniting the Mediterranean world in a single great system, as the Romans actually succeeded in doing four centuries later. Their failure was more a result of flaws intrinsic to Greek political values than of the strength and inventiveness of their enemies.

The Greek cities of Ionia had been subdued by the Persians in the late sixth century as part of a general plan to secure the northern and western frontiers of the Persian empire against possible barbarian invasions from the Balkans. The Persian conquest of western Asia Minor threatened the trade of the Greeks with their colonies on the Black Sea and gave cities such as Athens good reason to promote rebellion among the Ionians. By 494 B.C. the Ionian city of Miletus, which had rebelled against Persian rule, was subdued and its population deported. The Persian king Darius then moved against the Greeks on the mainland, banking not only on his superior force but also on the divisions among the Greek cities. When the Persian invasion was finally launched in 490 B.C., Greek resistance was organized with only indifferent success at first. Nevertheless, an Athenian army under the command of Miltiades met the Persian force at Marathon and repulsed it with extremely heavy losses.

A period of ten years' restive peace followed, owing to the death of Darius and the necessity of his successor, Xerxes, to put down revolts against Persian rule in Babylonia and Egypt. Then, in 480 B.C., a new Persian attack was mounted. This time most of the Greek cities joined in the defense of Hellas, although Sparta sent only a small force and Thebes defected to the Persians—an augury of things to come. The Athenians, however, had discovered rich silver deposits in Attica; with this new wealth and their commercial resources, they were able to purchase both ships and allies for the second great encounter with their Persian foes.

When the Persian army descended upon Greece, the Athenians evacuated most of the population of their city to the nearby island of Salamis; although the city was sacked, a combined Greek fleet destroyed the Persian navy at the battle of Salamis (480 B.C.) and saved the Athenian populace from destruction. In 479 B.C. the Persian army, which had wintered in northern Greece, attacked once more. This time the Athenians were joined by the Spartans; in two great battles, a land engagement at Plataea and a naval engagement at Mycale, the Persians were hurled back, and Greece was freed from further Persian pressures for over a half-century.

The Ionian cities now rose against their Persian masters and drove them from most of the coastal towns. Simultaneously, the Syracusans defeated the Carthaginians in a great battle at Himera (480 B.C.) in Sicily. The way was now open once more for expansion westward. Nothing seemed to stand in the way of the unification of the entire Mediterranean under Greek rule. Unfortunately, however, the unity that had been maintained (with only the greatest difficulty) during the time of the Persian invasion could not withstand the new pressures of peace and prosperity.

The vast wealth the Greek cities now enjoyed, combined with the sense of unlimited potential for expansion that now seized them, resulted in a renewed period of growth and experimentation, which lasted until 431 B.C. Many Greeks concluded that the new ideals and institutions that they had fashioned in the sixth century and that had become incarnated in the *polis* had withstood the severest test of all, contest with the mighty Persian Empire. Some of the leaders of the city-states, such as Pericles of Athens, faced the future with overriding self-confidence and the belief that man, now released from the trammels of convention, superstition, and tradition, could surmount any challenge presented to him. The Greeks had taken it upon themselves to form a social universe of order and justice on their own; they had succeeded; and they had overcome the threat of the "tyrannical" East. They expressed this new self-confidence and faith in man in a literary, artistic, and intellectual activity that made of the fifth century one of the greatest periods in world civilization. Unfortunately, however, the expansion in the range of their economic activity and their cultural vision was not accompanied by a commensurate expansion of their political perception. They remained wedded to the philosophy of political particularism. In the end, therefore, the egocentrism of the city-state triumphed over the potentiality for creating a world empire that their economic and intellectual inventiveness offered. The high enthusiasm of the post–Persian War period soon disintegrated into petty bickering among the victors, the creation of alliance systems for confiscating the spoils of the victory, and internecine strife, which weakened all of the cities of Greece. Persia profited from this division among the Greeks to consolidate her hegemony in the southeastern Mediterranean and looked forward to the time when she could return to Greece to redeem the honor lost in the Persian Wars.

THE PERIOD OF ATHENIAN HEGEMONY IN GREECE: 478–404 B.C.

Athens sought to claim the leadership of all Hellas in the years immediately following the Persian Wars. Many Greek cities, inspired by Athens' example, expelled tyrants and established democracies of the Athenian type.

Moreover, fear of possible Persian reprisals led many of these cities to unite behind Athens in a defensive alliance, the Delian League (478–454 B.C.), to which every member contributed money or ships to be disposed by Athens in the common interest.

But as the Persian threat diminished, many of the original members of the League sought to withdraw from it. Athens opposed these attempts, for Athenian statesmen recognized that any weakening of the League must weaken Athenian power in the Aegean and Black seas. Within two decades, Athens had begun to turn the resources of the League to her own purposes, on one occasion even employing the fleet to support an Athenian expeditionary force against the naval powers of the southeastern Mediterranean (459 B.C.). In 454 B.C. the Athenians removed the treasury of the League from the island of Delos to Athens and assumed the right to determine autocratically the uses to which the common funds were to be put. For example, Pericles used the League's funds to rebuild Athens in a style appropriate to the capital of a great, and expanding, empire. At the same time the rules of League membership were changed to Athens' advantage. For example, members were constrained to send money rather than ships or men and to allow Athens to provide out of her own industrial might and manpower the ships and sailors needed to man the fleet. These changes naturally resulted in feelings of resentment against Athens, especially in those cities whose main interests lay in trade with Italy and Sicily, where the Persian threat was virtually nonexistent, and in Ionia, which, prohibited by Athens from trading with Persia, was suffering from her protectors even more than she had at the hands of her persecutors. Therefore, many of the members of the League began to look to Sparta, the only independent major power on the mainland, for aid and protection; they tried to convince the Spartans that in the long run the Athenians were every bit as dangerous to Greek freedom and prosperity as the Persians had once been.

Sparta, however, had been hit very hard by earthquakes shortly after the close of the Persian Wars (464 B.C.); this disaster had been followed by a rebellion of the *helot* population (464–460 B.C.). The Spartans had more than enough to do to maintain internal security, and they preferred to remain uninvolved in anything that did not directly affect the state of affairs in the Peloponnesian subpeninsula. By 431 B.C., however, the Spartans realized that isolation was no longer possible—that Athenian growth must ultimately threaten Spartan hegemony in the Peloponnese.

The Athenian thrust towards Palestine and Egypt, led by Pericles and financed by funds drawn from the treasury of the Delian League, had failed. Now the Athenians turned envious eyes toward the rich farmlands of their sister cities in Sicily. The expansion eastward having been stopped, Pericles seems to have contemplated an expansion westward. Between Athens and Sicily, however, lay both Sparta and a number of cities on the northwestern coast of the Greek mainland that were either independent and desired to remain so or were linked by close bonds to Athens' commercial rivals, and especially to Corinth.

THE PELOPONNESIAN WARS: 431–404 B.C.

The immediate cause of the conflict between Athens and Sparta, which ultimately developed into the prolonged Peloponnesian Wars, was a dispute between a Corinthian colony, Corcyra (Corfu), and Corcyra's daughter city, Epidamnus, which enjoyed a position on the maritime trade routes to Italy and Sicily. In the course of the dispute, Epidamnus appealed for aid to Corinth, while Corcyra appealed to Athens. Sparta decided to back Corinth, and Pericles, now virtual ruler of Athens and ever a proponent of a strong imperialistic policy, opted for war. Soon all Greece was involved, and the cities of Ionia, the northern Aegean, Sicily, and southern Italy were ultimately drawn into the conflict. The war lasted, with intermittent periods of nervous peace, until 404 B.C. By the time it was finished, Athens had been ruined, Sparta weakened, and the whole of Greece so debilitated that it stood open to any foreign power ambitious enough to undertake the conquest. A series of wars involving Sparta, Corinth, and Thebes followed, to the disadvantage of them all.

The Athenians made a brief economic recovery in the first half of the fourth century, but they had lost all political direction and confidence. In the middle of the fourth century B.C., Athens tried to reestablish her empire, but unsuccessfully. The long period of warfare had critically weakened the Greeks, and in 338 B.C., a barbarian king from the north, Philip II of Macedon, conquered the entire Greek mainland and brought it under a single rule.

THE CAUSES OF GREEK DECLINE

Where had the Greeks in general and Athens in particular fallen short? The ultimate answer to this question cannot, of course, be given. But part of the answer seems to lie in the way in which the Greeks conceived human relations. Many Greeks appear to have believed that competition to the point of death was a rule of animal, and therefore of human, nature. The *polis* had been envisaged as an agreement between individuals and groups occupying a common ground to put aside competition with each other in order to direct their aggressions outward, against their neighbors in other cities and lands similarly organized. The Greeks failed to see that if competition were accepted as a general rule of human nature, it would be very difficult to deny that this struggle did not obtain *between the groups* making up the *polis* as well. The individual owed his loyalty to the *polis* only as long as he gained more advantages than disadvantages from serving it; it was conceivable therefore that in times of stress the rule of "every man for himself" might prevail.

The Delian League had been a confederation of cities that had pooled their resources—like the individuals in the cities—in the common interest of all. But when Athens' particular self-interest had been threatened, the Athenians denied responsibility to the group, rewrote the terms of confederation in their own best interests, and forced their allies to conform to their appraisal of the situation. Thucydides reports that when one of Athens' allies appealed to the principle of justice to support its claims against Athens' oppressive demands, the Athenian envoy answered by pointing out that the world was a jungle wherein the strong took what they wished and the weak suffered what they must.

Ultimately, that same rule came to prevail *in* Athens as well. Thus when Athenian fortunes began to decline, the various groups and individuals in the city began to abandon ship, as it were, each one saving what he could. The result was political chaos. But the citizens were merely following the rule they had been taught to observe during more prosperous and happier days: the strong were doing what they wished, and the weak were suffering what they had to suffer.

Therefore, whereas originally the city-state had offered a haven to the individual in a chaotic world, by the middle of the fourth century it had come to reproduce that chaos in a highly concentrated and especially oppressive way. In a social order where war was regarded as the rule rather than the exception, it is little wonder that men came to yearn for some supernatural power to deliver them. The exchange of freedom for stability seemed little enough to pay when freedom was identical with chaos.

THE MACEDONIAN TRIUMPH AND THE FOUNDATION OF HELLENISTIC CIVILIZATION

The defeat of Athens by Sparta, the subsequent wars between Sparta, Corinth, and Thebes, and the ultimate incorporation of Greece into the Macedonian Empire might have been fatal to Greek cultural development had the Macedonians been nothing but barbarians. But, rough as they were, the Macedonians had been imbibing Greek culture for some time prior to their conquest of Greece. Their king Philip was an admirer of Greek civilization, and his son Alexander had been taught by Greek masters, among whom was the philosopher Aristotle. Therefore, when Alexander (356–323 B.C.) succeeded his father in 336 B.C., the ground had already been prepared for a merging of Macedonian military vigor and Greek cultural sophistication. And when Alexander announced his decision to attack the Persians at the head of a Macedonian and Greek military alliance, he appeared to many Greeks merely to be carrying out the program that Pericles had unsuccessfully prosecuted over a century earlier.

But Alexander apparently had more in mind than a simple conquest of Persia; his fusion of Macedonians with Greeks in his army foreshadowed a greater plan, the amalgamation of the Greek and Persian cultures into a new, homogeneous civilization in which the best elements of each would be saved for general human benefit. Alexander's campaigns ranged as far east as northern India and southward into Egypt. His career from 334, when he first marched against Persia, to 323, when he died at the age of thirty-three, was a long series of military successes marred by increasing evidences of mental instability. He did not shrink from using terroristic methods to effect the synthesis of Greek and Persian culture, which had become his life's project since the death of his father.

His plan met with greater success with the Persians than with the Greeks, however. The former had long practiced cultural toleration, and they were not averse to living beside, and assimilating, alien cultural practices and traditions. But the Greeks seem to have begun to believe the myth of their own uniqueness; many of them regarded Alexander's assumption of Persian ways in dress, political administration, military technique, and the like, as evidences of an essential barbarism. Nonetheless, Alexander opened the way to a major infusion of Greek institutions, ideas, and people into the entire Near East. He built cities, encouraged colonization, forced intermarriage between his officers and Persian noblewomen, and promoted the use of Greek as an international language.

To provide a religious cement for this new cultural agglomeration, he took over the notion of the god-king, forcing even the Greek states to recognize him as the son of Zeus-Ammon. In the new empire that was to flourish under his divine rulership, political power would be vested, not in the individual *polis*, but in a monarch responsible to no one but himself. Thus Alexander proclaimed the death of the city-state as a viable *political* unit. In exchange for political stability, Greeks and Persians alike were to surrender political freedom; in return both would gain the economic and cultural advantages that only membership in a great empire could confer.

In fact, however, Alexander brought neither political stability nor economic prosperity to the lands he had conquered. His premature death cut short the execution of his grand design. Alexander did establish Greek culture in the Orient, and he did open up Greece to the influence of the East in religion, politics, art, and philosophy. But the Greco-Persian civilization that took shape after his death, which we call "Hellenistic," had more in common with the older Mesopotamian traditions than with those of Greece during its golden age.

The failure of Alexander's program was signaled by the terrible wars that ravaged the entire Near East for better than two centuries after his death. His generals, unable to agree on a single successor to their brilliant leader, carved up the empire into three major areas, conforming to the Greek, Mesopotamian, and Egyptian substrata on which Alexander had tried to impose a common *Greco-Persian* form. The Greek part of Alexander's empire fell to the general Antigonus, who founded a dynasty that ultimately centered in Macedonia and contended for control of the Aegean for the following century and a half. The general Seleucus founded a similar dynasty, which ruled over the Tigris-Euphrates valley, Syria-Palestine, and much of Asia Minor. The general Ptolemy established his line in Egypt. The three empires thus founded waged wars with each other, and with the various subject principalities that sought to win freedom from them, for the next two centuries. Their incessant wars weakened them and bred in their subjects an ardent longing for peace and stability. Thus it was a relatively easy matter for the Romans, when they finally turned to conquest in the East, to make short work of them. Macedonia and Greece fell to the Roman legions in 146 B.C.; the remnants of the Seleucid Empire were assimilated to Roman rule in 64 B.C.; and Ptolemaic Egypt succumbed to the power of Augustus Caesar in 30 B.C.

The conquest of Greece by Macedonia and of Persia by Alexander's combined Macedonian-Greek force marked the end of Hellenic civilization properly so-called. The main achievements of Greek civilization had been produced by men organized in autonomous city-states. When the city-states lost their autonomy, Greek culture lost much of its original creative tension and power. Although there were some attempts to restore Greek independence after the Macedonian conquest, few Greeks genuinely believed that the city-state was any longer capable of carrying out the program for which it had originally been founded: to provide justice to the individual and security for the group. Loss of faith in the city-state meant loss of faith in the ability of men—unaided by some kind of supernatural power—to build a life adequate to human needs. Thus the decline of the Greek city-state was accompanied by a revival of religious feeling, manifested above all by appeals for salvation to supermen, heroes, or agents of the gods to do what ordinary men were incapable of doing.

Greek acceptance of Alexander's claim to godhood signaled the political bankruptcy of Greek humanism. The formation of the city-states had been, in certain respects, a product of a rebellion against the old gods. When the city-state crumbled, the rebellion against the gods crumbled with it. Just as the Greeks of the fifth century B.C. had found justification for their rebellion in their success against the mighty Persians, so many Greeks of the fourth century B.C. saw their defeat by the Macedonians as a sign that their attempt at human autonomy had been presumptuous, even sinful, thus provoking the wrath of the gods. Under pressure of constant warfare, burdensome taxation, civil strife, and political corruption, the Greeks soon came to regard their cities less as guarantors of their freedom than as instruments of their punishment by the gods.

The Greek Cultural Achievement

By the end of the fourth century B.C., the Greeks had already lost much of their faith in men's ability to rule themselves and almost all of their confidence in the *polis* as the protector of human rights. But even then they did not lose their faith in man's ability to analyze and comprehend the human condition. Even as they watched with growing revulsion the disintegration of their political world, the Greeks continued to inquire into what had happened and was happening to them. Where had they gone wrong? What was there in human nature that appeared to turn every success into a failure? Had they actually been guilty of transgressing the limits set upon human aspiration by the gods, or had they merely miscalculated the material factors in worldly success and failure? Had the period of success been worth the labors that had originally brought it and the sufferings that had followed upon it?

If the Greeks had possessed the religious faith of the ancient Hebrews, who were suffering through similar catastrophes at about the same time, they would have had a ready answer for these questions. They would have concluded that their decline was due to some transgression of their covenant with their God, who was just, virtuous, and all-powerful, and who punished the wicked and rewarded the righteous according to His immutable law. But Greek religious traditions precluded any simple answer to these questions, and the philosophy that grew out of these religious traditions precluded any *single* answer.

GREEK PHILOSOPHY

Greek philosophy and the science that developed along with it were products of the Ionian Greeks' attempt to provide a rational and secular alternative to the religious idea of the world contained in Homer. The religion of Homeric times was intimately related to the tribal society of mainland Greece. When that society broke down under the impact of the Dorian invasions, the religion lost much of its relevance, especially to those Greeks who had migrated to Ionia and become urbanized. And so, sometime during the seventh century B.C., Ionian thinkers began to look for a plausible world-picture that would be at once congenial to the older religious ideas, on the one hand, and relevant to the new man-centered cultural life that had taken shape in the *polis*, on the other. Their point of departure was the conviction, expressed in Homer, that the universe was a system of processes governed by an immutable law. Homer had called this system *moira*, or fate. The Ionian philosophers progressively drained this concept of its anthropomorphic elements and defined it as a purely material system ruled by laws that were essentially rational and hence knowable to human reason, even if they were immutable and totally determinable of human, as well as other natural, activities.

Their strategy was to look for a primal substance, from which all others derived, and then try to determine the principles that would explain how this primal substance took on different forms in physical, animal, and human nature.

They began by identifying the primal stuff with what they thought of as the elements. The philosopher Thales (early sixth century B.C.) likened the primal stuff to water, presumably because it could assume the qualities of a liquid, a solid, or a gas; while the philosopher Heraclitus (*ca.* 500 B.C.) likened it to fire, since it was heat that effected the transformations of that water upon which Thales had based his interpretation. Yet another, Anaximenes (*ca.* 546 B.C.), held that the primal stuff was air, which, according to him, contained the opposites of both heat and cold, depending upon the speed at which it moved. Anaximander (*ca.* 550 B.C.) was the most abstract and theoretical of all: he called the primal stuff the infinite (*apeiron*), because it was no special thing but could take on the aspect of everything.

Anaximander's theory was similar to the theory that underlies much of modern science, since it turned the attention of the investigator to the *processes* by which things combine and break up rather than to endless speculation about the *ultimate nature of the world*. Yet the Ionians did not produce anything like modern science, with its technological orientation and its desire to translate *knowledge about nature* into *control over nature*. Instead they got lost in the question of why change occurred at all. For them, the interesting question was why, given the completeness and self-containedness of the primal substance, it apparently had to try to become something else.

One of the more fruitful answers to this question was suggested by Pythagoras of Samos (late sixth century B.C.), who argued that since the unity and autonomy of the primal stuff was self-evident, all of the transformations that men saw or thought they saw were only apparent, delusions, products of undependable sense perceptions. It thus seemed to Pythagoras that the investigator had to devise some means of disciplining the senses so that the unchanging stuff behind everything could be perceived and its true nature determined.

How was this to be done? Pythagoras held that differences between things were functions of different structures. He seems to have been encouraged to hold this position by his reflections on music and his realization that the differences between the various musical notes of a lyre depended, not on the material of which the strings were composed, but on the rates of vibration of the strings that produced them. Hence he concluded that true knowledge of the world consisted in the identification of the formal structures, mathematical in nature, that inhered within or existed behind things. This seemed to suggest a nonphysical, or spiritual, world knowable to the mind but not to the senses. Pythagoras thus set Greek philosophy on the way to the *idealism* that finally triumphed in Plato. He provided the basis of the theory that *Ideas* existed beyond the world of matter, in a sphere of changeless essences, and that the material world was only a pale and imperfect reflection of it.

Thus, Greek philosophical thought tended to divide between materialism and idealism. In Athens during the fifth century B.C. both of these traditions received their classic formulations. The philosopher Democritus (late fifth century B.C.) was the outstanding materialist. He maintained that the world was composed of tiny bits of matter (atoms), which came together in different combinations according to certain laws to create different things out of the single material substance. Plato (*ca.* 429–347 B.C.) represented the alternative idealist position. For him—as for Pythagoras—the material world could hardly be said to exist at all, and the philosopher's task was to penetrate through it to the changeless world of Ideas beyond.

The split in Greek philosophy ran parallel to a split in Greek religion. In the seventh century B.C. a new religion from Asia Minor, Orphism, had gained converts all over Greece. This religion, in contrast to the Homeric one, preached the uncleanliness of the flesh, spoke of a dark river of energic forces that underlay the superficial order of earthly life, and taught the necessity of liberating the inner spirit of mankind from the prison of the body on ritual occasions. Insofar as Orphism set up a dualism between body and spirit, it seemed to resemble Pythagorean philosophy; there is some speculation that Pythagoras's work was essentially only a secularized form of Orphism, just as Ionian philosophy may be regarded as a secularized form of Homeric theology, and especially of the concept of fate.

The metaphysical turn of Greek thought worked against a resolution of the quarrels that divided Greek philosophers into contending schools. They could not, like modern scientists, appeal to empirical data to establish their theories; for, increasingly, empirical data themselves were regarded by the Greeks as a problem to be explained rather than used as evidence. While this turn in Greek philosophy discouraged the development of a science of the modern sort, it did much to encourage the development of the tools of logical discourse and debate.

One group of thinkers in particular, called Sophists, led by Protagoras of Abdera (mid-fifth century B.C.), studied and taught the methodology of argumentation with especial subtlety. In modern parlance a sophist is one skilled in argumentation, one who can, and will, defend any position, without regard for a presumed absolute truth or universal ethical values. But the Greek Sophists should not be thought of as mere propagandists or public-relations men, as they are sometimes represented. They were educators who believed that human knowledge was a tenuous and imperfect acquisition and who were interested in determining how human thought was influenced by the time and place in which it arose.

Because they were relativists in thought, they tended to be relativists in moral matters as well. That is, they were inclined to relate every proposition or belief about morality to the social environment in which it was formulated. They did not believe in absolute ethical truths or ideals, but they were not—on the whole—socially irresponsible men, for all that.

The Sophists believed that human culture was at bottom a product of human speech, that speech was in turn a product of chance social and natural factors, and that knowledge could not be separated from the language in which it was expressed. They were therefore well suited to serve as the educators of the sons of the upper classes of the Greek cities during the fifth century B.C., for they stressed "practical" education in politics, commerce, and social life. When the cities in which they were teaching were democratic in spirit, they educated the young to participate in democratic political practices. When, however, the political climate was not democratic, the Sophists' educational philosophy required that they turn their talents just as ardently to the creation of the kind of citizen who could prosper in an aristocracy, oligarchy, or tyranny. They were, in short, politically neutral, or so they believed. Needless to say, their political neutrality could be used by those who desired to undermine the *status quo*, whatever it might be; for the students of the Sophists were often less interested in accommodating to the *status quo* than in manipulating it in their own self-interest. And here "neutrality" could very easily degenerate into cynicism.

Socrates (*ca.* 469–399 B.C.) was an outspoken critic of the Sophists, yet in the method that he used to train his own students, he was also the Sophists' continuator. Plato suggests that Socrates believed that knowledge was possible only on the assumption that a changeless sphere of essences—ideal goodness, truth, and beauty—existed behind the changing world of appearances. Thus he taught, in opposition to the Sophists, that there was no such thing as a morally neutral act and that men ought not merely adjust to things as they found them, but consciously strive to do the good in everything, regardless of the immediate practical consequences. But the dialectical method that Socrates used to establish this position was Sophistic in its origin: this method stressed close analysis of the progression of an argument, the confrontation of opposed views within a position held, and exposure of inconsistencies within a position that appeared to be, at first glance, both self-evidently true and internally consistent. Using this method, Socrates' student, Plato, criticized the philosophy and the politics of the age of the Peloponnesian Wars. In his criticism he likened the corrupt politicians he saw flourishing around him to the Sophists: both were more interested in profiting from the chaotic situation than in changing it, or so Plato believed.

THE CARE OF THE INDIVIDUAL:
GREEK MEDICINE AND EDUCATIONAL THEORY

None of this should be interpreted as suggesting that the opponents of the idealists, the materialists, were not concerned with moral issues. Quite the contrary. In fact,

Greek medicine—Ionian in its origins—provided fruitful models on which a materialistic theory of the healthy society could be constructed. For example, the Greek physician Hippocrates, a contemporary of Socrates, envisaged the human organism as a material system which, in its essence, was perfectly balanced. Sickness and disease Hippocrates attributed, not to the gods, but to the entry into the body of foreign elements or humors, which upset the harmonious balance of the air, earth, fire, and water that made up the host organism. When the organism fell ill, he believed, the physician's primary task was to help it to recover its natural balance. This was done by isolating the body, by placing it in a neutral—that is, sterile—environment so that it could carry on its struggle with the alien element and discharge it without distraction or diversion. In Hippocrates' view, nature was its own best physician, and it naturally tended toward harmony and health. Once the natural balance was restored, the organism could function creatively in its normal environment.

The fundamentally contemplative and passive nature of Greek science can be seen in the Hippocratic method. Even in their most materialistic moments, the Greeks did not believe that nature could be manipulated or altered in the way the modern technological scientist believes that it can. In short, Greek science was *accommodative* rather than *manipulative*. The task of the scientist was to discover the rules governing the universe or an organism in the universe. Once he had found them out, the scientist was to use this knowledge to distinguish between those areas where positive action on the part of men was possible and those areas in which mechanical necessity ruled. This was as true in what we would today call physics and chemistry, as it was in biology and medicine. For the Greek, the aim of human knowledge was to discover where and under what conditions human effort could be profitably undertaken. The purpose of human action was to do what was possible, not change the world.

It is easy to see how this Hippocratic theory of the role of the physician paralleled the psychological and social theories of the Greeks. Philosophers, especially the Sophists and Socrates, spoke of themselves as "midwives" of thought. They were doing in the sphere of the mind what the physician was doing for the body—that is, allowing the mind to express itself "naturally" clearing away confusions that blocked its normal operations.

Socrates' educational theory was founded on the belief that the teacher could only bring out ideas and abilities already present within the individual at birth. Socrates did not see it as the purpose of the teacher to teach rules and information to the student. Since the student could learn only what he in effect already knew, the teacher, like the physician, had to create a neutral environment in which the student could come to know himself, what he was capable of, and what he ought to do with his life. This was done by subjecting the environment to criticism in such a way as to liberate the individual from thoughtless conformity to its prejudices and the conventional wisdom. The hope was that the student would ultimately become a creative member of his society, but creative precisely in the degree that he had rid himself of all illusions about both the society and himself.

Naturally, the teacher who proceeded on such assumptions was highly valued during periods of political self-confidence and economic prosperity, but was often regarded as subversive when the society was under stress. During periods of crisis, Greek society tended to view a teacher like

Socrates as the *cause* of the breakdown of the family, the state, and religion, rather than as healer and truth-seeker. And during such periods political leaders ordered the teacher to teach patriotism and conformity to what the state demanded of its citizens. When he did not do so, the teacher was criticized, harassed, and—as the case of Socrates shows —occasionally driven from the city or executed.

THE NATURE OF THE SOCIAL PROCESS: GREEK HISTORICAL THOUGHT

The notion of the physician-educator was carried over into Greek politics by the conception of the politician as one who mediated between conflicting interest-groups in the state, maintained balance between the various elements in society, and disposed the state's power with a minimum of friction. In one of Plato's dialogues, Socrates claims that he is a better politician than Pericles because whereas he, Socrates, always worked for the good of society as a whole, telling the Athenians truths they could not comfortably entertain, Pericles merely played up to their prejudices in order to remain in power—and led Athens to disaster.

This opinion of Pericles was not shared by Socrates' contemporary, the soldier-historian Thucydides (*ca.* 460– *ca.* 400 B.C.), who wrote a classic account of the Peloponnesian Wars. Thucydides seems to have been strongly influenced by Hippocratic ideas, and he represents Pericles as a kind of political physician, the makeweight of political balance and health. He saw the decline of the Athenian state as a result of the triumph of extremists who had thrown Pericles' program of cautious expansion to the winds, had exceeded the natural limits of Athens' power, had created imbalances in the Athenian social order, and had then tried to salvage what they had ruined by the "total solution" of the Sicilian expedition.

In Thucydides, Greek historical thought produced its greatest genius. His story of the first decades of the Peloponnesian Wars is not only our principal account of that event, it has remained a veritable model of a scientific mode of historical analysis for over two thousand years. Like Hippocrates, Thucydides rejected the notion that the breakdown of an organism, whether physical or political, could be attributed to the gods, fate, or some moral principle underlying the whole of reality. For him, Athenian society was a victim of generally comprehensible natural processes and the psychological by-products of the social organism's reactions to its condition. To Thucydides, Athens was a complex of material and human potentialities, which, by a combination of chance and human planning, had hit upon a successful social order that allowed virtually unlimited growth and progress, if balance within it and between it and its environment could be maintained. The Periclean gamble for empire was neither moral nor immoral; it was "natural," given Athens' power and the opportunities presented to her.

Where Athens went wrong, Thucydides held, was in the loss of reason caused by the great plague that broke out during the second year of the war with Sparta. The plague had been unexpected, and no ready remedy for it could be found. The hysteria caused by the plague's impact resulted in the public's loss of self-confidence, in the dismissal of Pericles, and in the rise to power of extremists who played upon the public's fears and promised simple solutions for complex problems. With the failure of each of these proposed solutions, the parties vying for power became more irrational, more desperate, and more inclined to gamble on even more senseless projects. Once the plague had hit,

Thucydides concluded, Athens' defeat appeared foreordained, but not because the gods or fate had willed it; rather, because men, being what they were, were naturally frightened by anything new and unexpected and tended to act irrationally in the face of it. But the outcome had not been inevitable, Thucydides thought. If men like himself would record the experiences of the war realistically, make clear the reasons for Athens' failure, and save her experiences to human memory, it might be possible for other men at other places to avoid Athens' fate in the future.

Thucydides' predecessor, the so-called father of history, Herodotus (early fifth century B.C.), had approached history in a similar spirit, although he had intended to be more of a simple story-teller, a literary artist, than a scientist. Herodotus was interested in explaining the decline and fall of another great power, Persia, at the hands of the apparently poor and weak, yet talented, Greeks. In the course of his researches Herodotus traveled over the entire Near East, gathering information, recording stories, tales, myths, legends, and accounts of religious ceremonies and political institutions wherever he could find them. His main purpose was to entertain the irrepressibly curious Greeks with accounts of strange facts and exotic events. But he had a deeper purpose as well: to determine the causal principle by which changes in the social and political sphere occur. Like his Ionian scientific predecessors, he was convinced that comprehensible physical principles underlay all change, including social change, and he thought he knew what that principle was: the world was a balance or harmony, and extreme or excessive movement in it upset that balance, requiring the redisposition of all the forces in the system to their "natural" places in order to restore it to health.

The history of the Persian Empire, Herodotus seems to say, confirmed the principle expressed in such popular sayings as "what goes up must come down." The Persians, blinded by fascination with their own success to the fundamental rule of the universe, had gone beyond the limits set for them by the cosmic system. Their pride kept them from seeing the warnings contained in a number of minor failures. Every failure had prompted them to greater and greater efforts, until at last they had so overweighted their investment in world conquest that the entire universe had responded by allowing the Greeks to defeat them.

Thus, for Herodotus, the Greek victory over the Persians had not been a result of Greek virtue alone. The Persians had been the cause of their own defeat, the Greeks merely the instrument of the disaster. Of course, the perspicuity of the Greeks was shown by the efficiency with which they had exploited their chance of victory. But Herodotus's story of the fall of Persia was meant to remind those who came after them of the truth taught by Greek philosophy: that every aspiration involved a risk, that the higher one rose the deeper one fell, and that when critical self-consciousness gave way to blind impulse, the entire cosmos was offended and acted to right the balance thus upset, without regard for the motives or intentions of the actors. This was the same message, presented as a principle governing individual no less than general social and physical phenomena, of Greek tragedy.

THE PROBLEM OF HUMAN SUFFERING:
GREEK TRAGEDY

The most original creation of the Greek literary genius was tragic drama, which, like Greek philosophy and science, seems to have been, in both informing insight and performance, originally a secularized form of a religious tradition. It was influenced especially by the Dionysiac religion, the cultic purpose of which was to help the soul transcend its bodily limitations. This is the central problem of all tragedy: the conflict, not between good and evil, but between two processes, each equally valid and necessary to the world order, which converge and meet in man, and destroy him.

It is sometimes said that the subject of all tragedy is fate or destiny, the inexorable process that catches man up in its operations and senselessly grinds him to nothingness. Yet fate thus conceived is not the real subject of Greek tragedy; it is man's encounter with fate and the meaning or reason for man's suffering that are its true subjects. The idea of fate is necessary to the tragic vision in that not only is both the character, or excellence (*arete*), of the hero given to him by genetic endowment, but the circumstances that force an encounter between the hero and his society, nature, or the gods are themselves products of the entire world-process. Thus the view underlying Greek tragedy resembles Darwinism or Calvinism in the assumption that everything, both individual and general (social and physical), is part of an autonomous and rigorously consistent, all but mechanical, process. Seen from above, from the point of view of the tragic dramatist, this process has no breaks or discontinuities; tragedy assumes that the entire cosmos is self-consistent. But what interests the tragedian is the effect of the operations of the total process on the individual and the social consciousness. As in epic poetry, in tragedy the action is always seen from two points of view simultaneously, from that of the operations of the total mechanism as perceived by the gods, who know what the fates have decreed for man even though they cannot change it; and from the point of view of the hero, who is led to his doom in that process as the result of his possession, in excess, of some specifically human quality.

A heroine such as Sophocles' Antigone, for example, possesses the virtue of familial piety, which, when she is prohibited from burying her dead brother by the decree of the king of her city, becomes manifested in an excessive willfulness that blinds, not only her, but all about her, to any possibility of resolving the resultant conflict short of violence. Like the Persian Empire in Herodotus's history, Antigone is led to her doom by a virtue that would have been totally praiseworthy, had the situation not required that it be expressed in an extreme form.

Yet tragedy does not exhaust its potential as an art form by its examination of the operations of excessive virtue. It goes on to raise the question of why it should be that the cosmos, which through fate allots to each his portion of virtue or vice, *requires* human suffering. And in the greatest tragic writers of the fifth century, Aeschylus and Sophocles, it provides an answer: the hero must suffer so that the laws that govern the cosmos can become known to human consciousness in general. Thus envisaged, a tragic hero, such as Oedipus or Antigone or Orestes, is a kind of sacrificial lamb, who, because of an excess of human qualities, is the sole possible instrument for the growth of man's knowledge about his true nature and a universe of which he would otherwise remain completely ignorant, like an animal. Because the hero exists and suffers, the nature of the physical world and of the human condition in particular is made clearer and more comprehensible.

Thus Greek tragedy, properly understood, is a kind of passion play dedicated, not to the glorification of the gods, but to the creative powers of man—to the understanding of how those powers function, of the nature of their

conflict with the indifferent universe around man, and of
the progress of man in his contest with the universe.

Aeschylus (525–456 B.C.), who wrote in the buoyant
atmosphere created by the Athenian triumph over Persia,
used the tragic drama as a means of instructing the Athenian people about the nature of their achievement in found-
ing a city where human justice and law prevailed. His *Ores-
teia* ends with a hymn of praise for the newly established
Athenian law courts, where men were accorded a purely human protection from a chaotic world of nature. It was also
a means of explaining the larger mechanism that had led
the Persians to their doom even beyond the possibilities set
by Athenian civic virtue. In *The Persians* the pride of the
Persian kings is seen as the instrument that drives them
ever onward to greater and greater expansion, until they
overextend themselves and come to grief in Greece. On the
other hand, Sophocles (496–406 B.C.), who wrote during the
Periclean period of imperial expansion, examined the conflicts that were still possible even *within* the good society
and *between* the good society and the world around.

Superficially, the great tragic writers were merely
retelling the myths and legends that had come down to them
from Homeric times and before. But their true purpose
was to remind the populace of the inevitability of human
suffering, of the horror attending awareness of this suffering, even in the greatest of men, and of the fact that human
salvation, if it existed at all, existed as a common achievement of all men linked together in a struggle against
a world that offered them no aid whatsoever.

In plays like *Antigone* and the *Oedipus* cycle, Sophocles reminded the populace that suffering, if honestly confronted and contemplated, could be illuminating and liberating to human consciousness. The suffering of the hero,
thus envisaged, provided men with a reason to continue as-

piring even in the face of the knowledge that their suffering had only a human significance, led to no reward in the
afterlife, and prefigured no perfect paradise on earth.
Sophocles thus sought to dispel dispair and to inspire the
exercise of human virtue with moderation. This and this
alone, he believed, could lead to the creation of the best possible life for men on earth. Sophoclean drama therefore
sought to save the profits of suffering to consciousness,
forced men to recognize the implacable forces that opposed
them, and gave them models (heroes) on which to base
justification of their own aspirations—even against the gods
themselves.

The third of the great tragedians, Euripides (485–
?406 B.C.), writing during the desperate days of the Peloponnesian Wars, was less hopeful of human possibilities for
creative thought and action than was either Sophocles or
Aeschylus. He deals with characters who lack both a com-
prehension of the situation in which they find themselves
and any genuinely heroic impulses within themselves. He is
above all a psychologist, concerned with the power of the
passions over the conscious life. He shows that even when
men know the good, they do not always do it; he increasingly
sees men as pawns of dark processes that exist both within
and without them, which drive them to excess in everything,
and which ultimately destroy both the weak and the strong,
without any corresponding illumination or liberation of
those who surround the hero.

Euripides was disdainful of traditional Olympian religion but sympathetic to the concepts of the irrational contained in the new, and rapidly growing, Orphic religion.
For Euripides the "dark forces" were in the ascendancy.
He himself was exiled for impiety, but his impiety was
similar to that of Socrates—an attempt to educate the
Athenians to the dangers of merely ritual belief in the no-

bility of man, which threatened to lead them to their destruction. The idea of man's nobility had to be tempered,
Euripides seems to say, with a realistic awareness of the
ultimate power of those forces against which men had la-
bored for so long and which now gave every evidence of destroying them. Overwhelming evidence of the ascendancy of
these destructive forces was offered in the life and death of
Socrates, whose career was a kind of tragic drama played
out, not on the stage, but in real life.

SOCRATES

Socrates was the most famous teacher in Athens, a
friend and confidante of the ruling classes, and a political
educator of three generations of Athenian youth. But his
outspoken criticism of Athens' rulers in the aftermath of
the Peloponnesian Wars resulted in his being charged with
impiety towards Athens' gods and with corrupting the
youth. When found guilty, he was condemned to death, apparently with the tacit assumption that he would be allowed
to escape to go into exile.

But Socrates refused to play the game as it had been
set up for him. On the one hand, he pointed out, he had to
place the demands of his own conscience over the demands
of a social system that forbade him to do as he thought
right. On the other hand, he could not, he said, forsake the
city that had nurtured him. He could serve both his conscience and his city only by complying with its judgment
upon him. If he was wrong in what he believed about his
duty to his conscience and if the city was right, he deserved
to die. If he was right and the city was wrong, then the city
ought to change its ways.

His death in 399 B.C. was interpreted by his students,

especially Plato, as demonstrating that the democratic city-state had degenerated beyond redemption. Plato concluded that a society that was incapable of recognizing a man like Socrates as one of its greatest assets was not a guarantor of humanity but its enemy. When a man of Socrates' virtue could remain true to both himself and his city only by destroying himself, then the city that had condemned him had manifestly ceased to fulfill its function as a liberating institution and had become nothing but a power mechanism, unworthy of the loyalty of its citizens.

Inspired by Socrates' example, Plato spent the rest of his life investigating the conditions under which both freedom and order were possible. The older he grew, the more he became convinced that men had to choose between the two. Finally, he decided that order was preferable to freedom, if the choice had to be made. In his increasing authoritarianism Plato reflected the general drift of Greek thought in the fourth century B.C. Everywhere men were seeking some agency to relieve them of the burdens of freedom and autonomy; everywhere they were looking for someone or something to make their decisions for them, to give them a goal, and to discipline them when they failed to keep their gaze upon it.

GREEK THOUGHT AFTER SOCRATES: PLATO AND ARISTOTLE

As noted above, the death of Socrates in 399 B.C. signaled the death of Athenian democracy. The thinkers who succeeded Socrates in Athenian intellectual life were no longer interested in salvaging democracy so much as in salvaging from total chaos whatever they could of man's capacity for creative thought and action. Plato, especially, considered the problem of how, given what had been revealed about man's capacities for self-destruction in the Peloponnesian Wars, society itself could be saved. In his *Republic* he sought to construct a model of the ideal state against which every real state could be measured in terms of the degree to which it promoted or discouraged "the good life" idolized by earlier thinkers. Behind the composition of the *Republic*, however, there was another, more general motive: to determine to what extent human reason could be used to destroy the opinion, steadily growing in Athens, and Greece in general, that the state was *nothing but* a means of organizing sheer power drives and was founded on force, greed, and deception alone.

Plato's ideal state is conceived on the model of his conception of the individual human being. Justice in the ideal state Plato defines as the harmonious balance of *specialized classes*, each representative of some human virtue, present in equal measure in the ideal man. The *philosopher class* represents wisdom and is charged with the direction of the state; the *soldier class* represents courage and is charged with its defense; the *class of workers* represents temperance and is charged with the task of providing material sustenance for all.

The proper disposition of tasks in the ideal city falls to the philosopher class, although membership in that class is open to any with natural talent sufficient to the exercise of its functions, whatever the class membership of his parents. When each man is doing what he is best suited for, in accordance with the powers peculiar to him, justice rules the city, just as when, in the individual, wisdom, courage, and temperance are properly blended, virtue is the result.

The state imagined by Plato has been called totalitarian. And it is true that Plato conceives the social whole as greater than the sum of the parts. He notes that the part (the individual) could not exist without the whole (the city-state), whereas the reverse is possible. Hence the city is justified in demanding everything from the individual, since in effect it makes it possible for an individual to become a man—that is, to live the good life. Only in the relative security of the city can man realize whatever potential for virtue he has.

But to call the Platonic state totalitarian without qualification would be to do Plato an injustice. He was living at a time when it was thought that men had to choose between a life in society and no *human* life at all. Plato could not countenance a social order based upon material self-interest, because such a social order would have been, in his view, not a human order, but merely an animal one. He thought it necessary for most of humankind to choose between being disciplined by an intellectual elite, on the one hand, and being free, without the benefits of social intercourse with men, on the other. And he did not hesitate to choose the former alternative.

There was yet another reason why Plato believed that a state organized along the lines suggested in the *Republic* would be superior to anything that had been tried in Greece up to his time. As noted earlier, Plato was an idealist, an heir of the Pythagoreans, who believed that knowledge was possible only with respect to the changeless sphere of perfect forms. To him the senses were deceiving, and the capacity to penetrate through the changing world of appearance to the changeless sphere of perfect goodness, beauty, and truth was the perquisite of a small elite of intellectuals trained in mathematics, music, astronomy, and philosophy. Most people, he held, were not capable of living without the myths of traditional religion, and it was a mistake to try to liberate everyone from the restraining fear of the gods. Therefore, like many intellectual elitists who came after him, he advocated an aristocracy of talent rather than an aristocracy of blood, money, or strength, and proposed a system of thought control that would carefully shield the unworthy from exposure to uncomfortable truths about the nature of the universe.

Only the intellectual elite, Plato held, were capable of living in the cold, hard world of perfect, yet indifferent, forms. Only they possessed the self-discipline to pursue knowledge of those forms in a completely disinterested manner. Only they, therefore, should have the power of deciding in the sphere of practical affairs what would be beneficial to the city and what would not. There was no such thing as a science of politics, Plato held; it was a craft or at best an art. But the only men capable of practicing that art were those whose main interest was the higher realm of the spirit, that realm reflected best in the objects studied by mathematicians and astronomers: numbers and the stars.

Plato's student, Aristotle (384–322 B.C.), was less of an idealist than his master and less sanguine about the possibility of building a good society. He preached realistic compromise with the *status quo* and the mastery of human knowledge in all branches of learning as a means of attaining *individual* self-sufficiency. It was true, Aristotle taught, that perfect knowledge was possible only of abstract ideas, and men ought to strive for such knowledge. The spheres of human ethics and politics were subject to the vagaries of human choice, fear, impulse, and, therefore, chance. This meant that there could be no true science of them. The best that one could do was study how men had acted in different situations, construct models of the various *forms of action* that recurred in human affairs, and seek out that situation in which a man could flourish most easily.

The city-state was still necessary for human life, Aristotle believed; the man who did not live in the city was no better than an animal, a barbarian. For Aristotle the city existed to produce the circumstances in which the highest kind of individual, the philosopher, could exist and thrive. Such an individual required slaves and business men to provide him with physical necessities and luxuries; he required politicians to order the social sphere. But the ideal man is not himself either slave, business man, or politician, for all of these callings require involvement in some kind of animal exertion. All of them force the individual to choose between animal self-interest and the interest of the group to which he belongs. Only in the contemplative life of the philosopher is it possible to serve others by serving oneself; for in the pursuits of goodness, truth, and beauty, the philosopher contributes to the general good of his community in precisely the same degree that he contributes to his own good.

Having grown to manhood during the death-gasp of the *polis*, Aristotle knew that it was no longer the autonomous and self-sustaining entity that earlier thinkers had thought it was. If the city was to survive at all, it was necessary that some power be elevated over it, one that could keep the various cities from destroying one another, and, with them, civilization. Thus Aristotle encouraged his student, Alexander of Macedon, in his project of creating a great world-state, although he seems to have been more than disappointed in the form Alexander's empire assumed as Persian influences began to predominate over him. In the end, Aristotle taught that men had to make the best of an imperfect social existence. They had the world of nature on which to exercise their minds and the world of art on which to exercise their imaginations. They were well advised, therefore, to develop critical knowledge of both science and art, so as to better weather the storms of life with a maximum of pleasure and a minimum of pain.

PHILOSOPHY AND RELIGION
IN HELLENISTIC TIMES

Aristotle thus provided one point of departure for the development of the main traditions of thought and learning during the Hellenistic period. The Stoic school of philosophy taught, as Aristotle did, that the ideal man was self-sufficient, but it denied that self-sufficiency could be expressed in the mere pursuit of bodily or aesthetic pleasure. To the Stoics, life was hard and men showed their humanity only in the measure to which they faced up to its harshness, carried out their social duties to the best of their abilities, and resisted any impulse to egoistic self-indulgence. The Epicureans, by contrast, held that since life had no ultimate meaning, men ought to train themselves to heighten whatever pleasure they were vouchsafed during their time on earth. Originally, the Epicureans intended this doctrine to be understood as an injunction to liberate oneself from all physical necessity and to cultivate the pleasures of the intellect. But as men grew more insecure and less certain of the value of intellectual achievement, the doctrines of the Epicureans were cited to justify pursuit of sheer material pleasure. Whereas the Stoics consistently taught that physical nature was *lawlike* in its operations and that men ought to comport themselves so as to make their lives as orderly as nature, the Epicureans sometimes taught this and at other times taught that knowledge of the world existed to heighten men's enjoyment of it.

The difference between the two philosophies was one of emphasis rather than substance. But increasingly Stoicism became the point of view of men who were still, without very much hope, trying to bring order out of the social chaos of Hellenistic life; while Epicureanism became the philosophy of those who, resigned to chaos, decided to consume their days in the pursuit of sensual pleasure.

A number of other philosophical schools took shape in Hellenistic times, reflecting in different ways the demoralization that had set in following the breakup of the *polis*. Among these were Cynicism, Scepticism, and Neo-Platonism. The first two reflected the essential pessimism of men who had lost all sense of direction in the sphere of human affairs. The last, Neo-Platonism, was a combination of the Platonic doctrine of ideas and the mystery cults that flourished in the Near East and had become popular in the Greek-speaking world after the Alexandrian conquest of Persia. The Neo-Platonists stressed the illusory character of material existence, but unlike Plato himself, they held out the possibility of escaping from this material existence by mastery of the sacred lore contained in the oriental religious cults, philosophy, and science. The Neo-Platonists studied the realm of the spirit, not in order to serve men, but in order to *escape* them. They hoped to win salvation by an *escape* into the world of spirit, where, they believed, an eternal life, free of all pain, would be given them.

But none of these philosophies provided very much solace to the ordinary man. All presupposed the material security and freedom of the philosopher's life. Moreover, they presupposed the intelligence and learning of the philosopher. The ordinary man required something more concrete, less demanding, and more hopeful than anything that the philosophers offered. They found what they wanted in the oriental mystery cults, which, like Orphism, explained human suffering in simpler terms, offered ritualistic escapes from this suffering, and promised life after death to those who performed the rituals correctly.

During Hellenistic times the most popular mystery cults were those associated with some mother-goddess, such as Ishtar or Isis, or those that taught the coming of a savior, such as Osiris or Mithra, to deliver man from the forces of darkness which threatened to consume him. The goddess cults usually invited the devotee to take solace in the love that the mother-figure offered to mankind and to await with patience and forebearance the time when death would unite him with the mother-figure. The savior cults invited the devotee to worship a hero-god who would protect him from the forces of evil and to look forward to a bodily resurrection after death, similar to the hero-god's resurrection after his own battle with the evil forces, as portrayed in the myths of the cult.

Both kinds of cults usually enforced certain dietary rules and required participation in certain rites as well as support of the priesthood and temple dedicated to the god. The rites were colorful and narcotic in their effects upon the participants, manifestly sensual, and appealing to the imagination of the distracted humanity that flocked to them. The cults were not in general exclusivistic, and they afforded a community of feeling and aspiration that took the place of the city-state, which had failed, and of the great empires, to which the individual felt little personal loyalty.

When it first appeared, Christianity seemed to be merely another of these mystery cults, and the Romans treated it as they did all the others. Only gradually did it dawn on them that in Christianity they were facing a new religious phenomenon. Yet Christianity itself was influenced by the mystery cults and, apparently, by Neo-Platonism. Given Christianity's original sense of its uniqueness, this influence was a testimony to both the power of the cults and their hold on the imaginations of their believers.

GREEK ART

It is always tempting, and almost always fatal, to try to *write* about the visual and plastic arts. The reason is that if artists felt that they could best express what they had to say in words, they would use words, and not paint, or stone, or some other nonverbal medium. But it is especially difficult to write, or even to talk, about Greek art; for Greek art was quintessentially sculptural, and sculpture cannot even be photographed easily, much less described verbally. Sculpture, like architecture, must be walked around and looked at from different angles; its scale and its context are as important as its shape. It is therefore not easily reproducible, even in photographs; and since it is nonverbal, it is all but impossible to say what it "means." Nonetheless, cultural history is based on the belief that all forms of thought and expression reflect something of a common apprehension of the world; so when we speak of Greek civilization we must try to characterize its art along with its philosophy, its literature, and its social style.

Most generally we are taught that Greek art was harmonious, serene, balanced; that it represented in stone that ideal form that Plato had sought in mathematics and astronomy. This is not untrue, but it is only partially correct; it applies only to certain periods of Greek artistic development and only to the work of certain artists in those periods. In reality, Greek art was as complex and as variegated as modern art; it celebrated form and harmony, but it also celebrated chaos. It held up the ideal to man, just as Greek tragedy did; but, like Greek tragedy, it also showed him the reality. Greek art was not so much, then, the art of harmony and balance, as a way of reminding men that harmony and balance were only temporary acquisitions, that there were as many disruptive forces in life as there were harmonizing ones, and that when man relaxed his vigil, the forces of chaos were waiting to take advantage of the situation and throw over whatever had been raised, in fear and trembling, as a monument to human aspiration.

First of all, it should be noted that Greek temples were not the diminutive, garage-size buildings that they appear to be in photography; they were often mammoth structures, though designed to fit into their milieus without appearing assertive or intrusive. In short, they are not distinguished, by their scale, from the monumental art of the ancient Near East, such as the pyramids and the Sphinx. Secondly, Greek temples were no more meant to be viewed from within than a Greek sculpture was; they were meant to be viewed from without. And so the problem of the Greek architect charged with designing a temple was to resolve the differences between the function of the building—that is, its function as a dwelling place of the idol of the god— and its external appearance, as a part of a total environment. This the architect sought to do by giving to the structure the appearance of a *continuation* of the natural milieu in which it was raised. The Greek building seems to "float" on the horizon between earth and sky, neither settling too comfortably into the ground nor rising too precipitously skyward, as the Gothic cathedral does. Using the post and the lintel, a straight piece laid across two upright columns, as the basic structural components, the Greek architect affirmed simultaneously the weight of material existence and the forces of growth and aspiration in all *living* matter. When the two forces were in balance, the human viewer might be reassured in his effort to find a haven in a seemingly chaotic world.

From the massive archaic buildings of Minoan times through the marvelously balanced structures of the Athenian golden age of the fifth century B.C., there is a progressive lightening of the stone with which Greek temples were built. In viewing the masterpieces on the Acropolis, the high ground around which Athens developed, we are still struck by the Greek architects' ability to give to the huge columns the suggestion of natural, organic thrust upward and to the weight resting upon them the appearance of perfect symmetry and balance. By removing the containing wall to a space inside the surrounding columns, the melancholy effect of matter's imperviousness is dispelled without being denied. The surrounding light and air circulate into the building, and the gaze of man is drawn inward, to the center of things where the mystery of being is housed.

A similar effect is achieved by Greek sculptors, who were able to charge stone itself with the throbbing vitality of life, energy, and spirit. Yet Greek sculpture of the golden age does not suggest any impulse to deny the flesh, any desire to escape, but only a desire to realize completely the potentialities of the human life-form for growth and self-sufficiency. This is true both of statues, which stand free of wall and niche, and of the friezes, which portray scenes of battle, the forum, or athletic games. The action portrayed in the friezes is usually complete within itself, just as the spirit that resides within the individual sculpture is comfortably at home in its material body. Unlike Gothic sculpture of the Middle Ages, which looks outward toward the viewer and invites his participation in an arduous inner, spiritual struggle, or which looks upward towards the spiritual sphere from which the individual is separated, Greek sculptures affirm by their self-containedness the ideal which all men may, if they choose, aspire to.

None of this is true of either the art that preceded the golden age or that that followed it in the Hellenistic period. The art of the Homeric age tended to be stylized and hieratic—that is to say, composed according to formulae or in response to ritual needs. The art of the seventh and sixth centuries B.C., for example, is much more stiff and formal, much more suggestive of the fatalism that governed the lives of both gods and men, as Homer portrayed it. The art of the Hellenistic age, by contrast, is much more turbulent, much more suggestive of struggle between body and spirit, which the mystery cults and Hellenistic philosophy took to be an unhappy truth about human existence. But it is the art of the golden age that has repeatedly seized the imagination of Western man. The art of the archaic period is too similar to that of the ancient Near East and that of the Hellenistic period too similar to that of the Western Middle Ages to merit our attention as distinctively Greek phenomena.

The Historical Importance of the Greeks

Nowadays it has become conventional to value the *whole* of Greek culture, from its remote Minoan origins to its late Hellenistic twilight, and to seek to find in all periods of its development a similar excellence. This is as it should be, for artistic merit, literary achievement, and intellectual sophistication can appear at any stage of any culture's evolution. Moreover, in the twentieth century we have come to view the genius of such collective achievements as myth, legend, and fable with the same sympathy that we formerly granted only to individually identifiable talents. Thus we may collect Greek vases of the archaic period with the same interest and delight as earlier antiquarians collected statuary and friezes of the golden age. And we may find a greatness in Hesiod equal to that of Sophocles, since we no longer expect all poets to attempt the same things and therefore use different criteria to evaluate them.

Nevertheless, the fact is that *as a historical phenomenon* it is Greek culture of the fifth century B.C. that constitutes the most original contribution to the thought and art of modern Western civilization. More particularly, it is Greek *thought and art* of the fifth century B.C. that is effective in modern Western cultural life, rather than Greek *practice*—political, religious, or social. The Greeks of that age, in their efforts to frame an ideal for themselves, succeeded in creating a paragon of humanistic values for all subsequent ages, a model of how men must view the world if they desire to create a "realistic" human culture here on earth.

During the early Middle Ages, the Hellenistic Greeks exerted strong influence on Christian culture through Neo-Platonism, which found its way into theology, via St. Augustine above all. During the late Middle Ages, Aristotle was called upon by Western thinkers to help them frame a theory of the world that was conformable to the demands of Christian theology on the one hand and to a new material reality on the other. Then, in the Renaissance, European thinkers went back to the fifth-century Greeks to find justification for their proposed revision of Western values in a humanistic sense. It is true that the Renaissance humanists were selective in what they borrowed from the Greeks; they valued Plato especially, but they were uncomfortable with the realistic Thucydides and tended to ignore his hard lessons in political theory.

It was not until the nineteenth century that historians, archaeologists, and philologists really turned to the task of reconstructing fifth-century Greek culture in all its variety and integrity. And it is only in our own century that we have come to appreciate the Greeks for what they were rather than for what we would like them to have been.

But there was one people who knew the Greeks intimately, valued them highly, and sought self-consciously to graft their own destiny onto that of the Greeks. This was the Romans, a people that had been building a stable political and social order in central Italy during the same time that the Greeks were flamboyantly and sporadically working at that task in Hellas. The Romans resembled the Greeks in many respects, but they differed from them in one important way: they successfully created the kind of cosmopolitan world-order of which only the most exceptional Greeks had even *dreamed*. When, during the second century B.C., the Romans finally began to expand their empire eastward, they encountered a world that had already been prepared to receive them by Greek efforts at imperial consolidation. They fell heir to a culture they had already come to know through contact with the Greek cities in southern Italy for many centuries. They embraced the ideals of Greek culture and used them to explain and to justify their own achievement. They were so successful at this confiscation that for centuries the Greek and the Roman achievements were looked upon as simply different aspects of the same single effort. There is some justice in this identification, but it should not obscure the fact that the Romans brought a genius uniquely their own to the creation of what we call classical humanism. It is to this genius that we must now turn.

ROME

The Emergence of Rome as a World Power

The Mediterranean basin is—like the Aegean, though on a larger scale—a natural communications unit. By the end of the fourth century B.C., most of its coastline was occupied by civilized peoples that were as much at home on the sea as they were on the land. The organization of all these peoples into a single political system by the Romans, therefore, has in restrospect the look of historical inevitability. But this is only in historical retrospect: when Rome emerged as a major power in the third century, no one, least of all the Romans, entertained the hope of organizing the entire Mediterranean world into a single polity. The age of the great empires had apparently passed forever with the failure of the last of the empire-builders, Alexander the Great. To the men who came after him the Mediterranean area must have seemed a crazy quilt of irreconcilable cultural traditions, peoples, monarchies, independent cities, and tribes, sharing little more than a common concern for survival. The sheer number of contending powers made unification difficult to conceive. And if it had been suggested that the Romans would be able to achieve what Alexander had failed to do, the idea would probably have been adjudged insane.

Actually, however, the very number and diversity of the contending powers in the late fourth century made unification more of a possibility than it had been in earlier times. Two centuries of wars, conquests, rebellions, and counterconquests had diluted the various cultural streams, and the strength of many was the weakness of all. In times when war is the rule rather than the exception, hegemony is often the prize of the nation that has best cultivated the art of survival. And survival was the Romans' special talent. The Romans neither consciously sought after, nor systematically organized, their empire as it took shape. They took up the task of imperial consolidation almost as an afterthought, as a burden that their many victories in wars of self-defense had foisted upon them.

THE POLITICAL SITUATION
IN THE THIRD CENTURY B.C.

At the end of the fourth century B.C., there were basically six major powers in the Mediterranean basin. The eastern half was the scene of a contest between the three monarchies that had emerged from Alexander's empire: Antigonid, Seleucid, and Ptolemaic. Greece was caught up in a struggle between the Antigonid kings of Macedonia and the old city-states now organized in leagues and trying to recapture something of their former wealth and power. This struggle weakened both parties so severely that the way was thrown open to invasion by barbarian tribes from the north. During the first quarter of the third century, the Celts streamed into Hellas. They sacked and looted at their pleasure, and Greece was saved only by the Celts' decision to pass over into Asia Minor, where they formed a kingdom of their own in Galatia.

At the same time, in the Fertile Crescent the Seleucid kings of Mesopotamia and the Ptolemies of Egypt contended for control of the Syria-Palestine corridor. Five so-called Syrian wars were fought between 276 and 195 B.C., all with inconclusive results. There was to be no peace for this troubled area until the first century B.C. when Rome arrived to subdue both parties. Even then peace was tenuous, for beyond Syria, further east, there had arisen in 248 B.C. yet another great power, the Parthians, who occupied a territory reaching from the Euphrates river into northern India. And not even the Romans could pacify the Parthians.

In the western half of the Mediterranean a similar situation obtained. There also three powers were contending for hegemony: Carthage, the Sicilian Greeks, and the Romans. Carthage, originally a Phoenician colony in North Africa (in present-day Tunisia), was the most powerful; it controlled a vast maritime empire with bases in Spain, France, Sardinia, Corsica, and Sicily. Some of the city-states in Greek Sicily had designs on parts of Italy, southern France, and North Africa, and during the fifth and fourth centuries they were constantly at war with Carthage. In the third century, however, the Greeks' fortunes declined, and Carthage threatened to absorb all of Sicily. When some of the Sicilian cities appealed to Rome for aid and Rome responded, the issue between Carthage and Rome was joined.

As for the Romans, throughout the fifth century they had been concerned primarily to consolidate their position in central Italy, against the Etruscans to the north and the Greeks to the south. In the long run, they had been eminently successful, but it had been a difficult task. The ancient Romans were not especially aggressive, but land-hunger had forced them to expand at the expense of their neighbors. Like the Spartans, therefore, they conquered surrounding lands. But because their immediate neighbors were themselves bounded by even more aggressive peoples, peoples who were potentially hostile to Rome itself, the Romans did not attempt—as the Spartans had done—to reduce their own neighbors to slavery. Although the Romans were not above using terror in subduing their enemies when they had to, on the whole they preferred to enlist them in alliances of one sort or another for mutual defense and protection.

Some of Rome's allies were bound to her by permanent contracts; others were granted full citizenship rights in the Roman commonwealth. Rome followed no specific rule in binding other cities and tribes to herself, but she always retained the right of directing foreign policy and of adjudicating disputes that arose between the different members of the confederation. Moreover, by the end of the fourth century, Rome had begun to link her allies to herself by a great web of roads, which made communication between the strategically important points of the Roman defensive system simple and efficient.

The strength of the Roman system was tested a number of times before the encounter with Carthage. In 387 B.C. a band of Celts from the north took Rome and sacked it, and in 321 B.C. the bellicose Samnites to the south destroyed a Roman army at Caudine Forks. Both misfortunes could have been disastrous; in both crises, however, the Roman confederation held firm. The eventual defeat of the Samnites, in 304 B.C., brought Rome face to face with the Greek cities in southern Italy. By 275 B.C. these cities had been incorporated into the Roman combine. The Romans now controlled all of Italy, save Cisalpine Gaul to the north and Sicily to the south. It was only a matter of time before they would come into open conflict with Carthage.

THE PUNIC WARS: 264–146 B.C.

The wars between Carthage and Rome are called the Punic Wars, from the Latin word for Phoenician, *Punicus*. The first of these wars, which lasted from 264 to 241 B.C., arose under circumstances similar to those that had caused the Peloponnesian War in Greece—that is, by appeals for aid to Carthage and Rome simultaneously by cities in Sicily. There were other similarities as well. Rome was—like Sparta—primarily a land power, dependent upon its army; Carthage—like Athens—was essentially a naval power whose strength depended upon control of the sea. But here the similarities ended. For Rome showed itself much more flexible than Sparta, much more able and willing to adjust to necessity. During the course of the First Punic War, for example, the Romans built a great fleet and defeated the Carthaginians on sea as well as on land. And at the end of the war, Rome took over Sicily, Sardinia, and Corsica, which forced her to become a naval power fit to contend with Carthage for complete control of the western Mediterranean.

The Carthaginians showed a similar creativity in defeat. They conquered Spain to the Ebro River, moved into southern France, and, finally, under the leadership of a great general, Hannibal, invaded Italy itself. This triggered off the Second Punic War, which lasted for eighteen years (218–201 B.C.) and all but devastated the Roman peninsula. Hannibal showed himself a master strategist and tactician, especially at the battle of Cannae (216 B.C.), where he destroyed a Roman army far outnumbering his own forces.

But Hannibal's military genius was no match for Roman diplomacy. He had banked on the defection of Rome's allies in Italy. But the Roman confederation remained solid, and he was forced to look to the East for aid. Hannibal's treaty with Macedonia involved Rome, whether she desired it or not, in the political affairs of Hellas. The first Macedonian War (215–205 B.C.) was fought by the Romans with the aid of an alliance of Greek cities. At the same time, the Romans carried the war to Spain. There they suffered repeated defeats before the arrival of the talented general Publius Cornelius Scipio (Scipio Africanus) in 210 B.C. Within a few years Scipio had driven the Carthaginians from Spain and invaded North Africa. This drew Hannibal home from Italy to organize the Carthaginian defense. In 202 B.C. Hannibal confronted Scipio in the battle of Zama, in which the Carthaginian army was annihilated. Hannibal escaped, but Carthage surrendered and was forced to cede Spain, the Balearic Islands, and her entire navy. Rome left Carthage nominally free but demanded payment of an annual tribute.

ROME IN THE EAST

Hannibal now took refuge with the Seleucid king Antiochus IV and tried to organize a league against the Romans in the East. During the Second Macedonian War (200–197 B.C.) the Romans, again aided by leagues of Greek cities, had to face both Macedonia and Syria. Victory in Hellas was followed by a war in Syria (192–189 B.C.) and another in Macedonia (171–168 B.C.). The Greek cities then took the opportunity offered by the general confusion to declare their independence from both Macedonia and Rome and called upon the Syrians to aid them. Ultimately, in order to put an end to the disturbances caused by Greek duplicity, the Romans incorporated both Macedonia and Greece into their empire.

Finally, fear that a revived Carthage might threaten Rome from the west led to yet a Third Punic War (149–146 B.C.). This war was unprovoked, and we may use it to mark the point at which Rome turned from the defensive to the offensive in the construction of an empire. The result of the Third Punic War was the destruction of Carthage and the extension of Roman power into North Africa. Other wars were fought in Macedonia, Sicily, and Asia Minor before the empire was definitively consolidated, but by 132 B.C. the empire was a fact even if it was not a fully articulated idea. Later, all of Syria, Palestine, and Egypt would also be incorporated into the Roman system as part of a conscious policy of imperial consolidation.

Little by little the Roman populace, descendants of an insignificant farming community on the banks of the Tiber, had conquered the entire Mediterranean world. The official legends proclaimed that the Romans had neither wanted nor anticipated such power as the empire gave them. But there was no turning back. The Romans now governed an area greater than that ruled over by Alexander the Great. And the question which now confronted them was, What were they to do with it? The Romans had backed into an empire in the defense of their own unique form of government. Now that they had defended themselves successfully, they had to consider whether their own empire was not a greater threat to the republic than the enemies they had had to defeat in defense of it. That they had never adequately confronted this question was shown by the effects that the empire had on internal affairs in Rome.

Early Rome: Tribal Origins and Early Institutions

The Romans belonged to the Latin branch of the Italic peoples, a group of Indo-European tribes that had drifted into the Italian peninsula from northern Europe around 1000 B.C. The Latins settled in villages on the plain of Latium in south central Italy. Sometime before the eighth century B.C., a number of Latin villages on the River Tiber coalesced to form the primitive Roman community. The land around Rome was rich, and the city was located on a trade route along which salt was transported from the mouth of the Tiber to the hill country of the interior. Rome's central position among the Latins, the Latins' central position in Italy, and Italy's central position in the Mediterranean help explain the power that Rome subsequently acquired in the ancient world. But these geopolitical considerations are only part of the story. Much more important were the ways in which the primitive Roman populace responded to pressures that bore in upon them from more highly civilized peoples around them, the Etruscans to the north and the Greeks to the south.

Shortly after the Latin settlement, the Etruscans, an oriental people possibly originating in Asia Minor, made their way to Italy and established themselves in Etruria (present-day Tuscany and Umbria). During the seventh century B.C., these Etruscans conquered all of central Italy, from the Po valley to Salerno, established their rule over the Romans, introduced them to advanced urban life, and imposed upon them cultural traditions that were to remain a part of Roman civilization ever afterward. The Etruscans influenced Roman religion and burial customs, and may have contributed to the Latin alphabet. And they gave the Romans certain conceptions of authority, or so it seems.

But the Etruscans also gave the Romans a profound distaste for kingship. And when the opportunity presented itself in 509 B.C., the Romans rebelled, expelled their Etruscan kings, and constituted themselves a republic. They vested a kind of monarchical power in the office of consul, two of which were elected annually, but for nearly five hundred years the Romans resisted all attempts to reconvert their republic into a monarchy. Even Julius Caesar hesitated to have himself proclaimed king, although he certainly considered the idea, and Augustus Caesar made himself a king only under cover of the mask of savior of the republic.

ROMAN REPUBLICAN INSTITUTIONS:
509–133 B.C.

However, Rome was an *aristocratic* republic from the beginning. The Romans distinguished between a noble class—the patricians, supposedly descended from aristocratic families of the tribal period—and a class of commoners, the plebeians. The original division of the people into what amounted to castes was to make for disruptive tensions during the first two centuries of the republic's existence. But because the liberation from Etruscan rule had been effected by the *whole* Roman people, patrician and plebeian alike, the republican form of government enjoyed an especial prestige among that people. In the end the republican form endured, and Rome entered onto the stage of world history less as a nervous innovator in political organization than as a self-confident carrier of a form of polity that had both its success and its antiquity to commend it.

The internal history of the Roman Republic down to

the middle of the second century B.C. can be characterized in the consideration of three factors in Roman civic life: the *fact* of class division between patricians and plebeians; the *idea* of the essential unity of the Roman people; and the *struggle* between the two classes for control of the principal offices of government.

When Rome became a republic in 509 B.C., the patrician class assumed direction of Rome's political destiny. The representatives of the patriciate met in the Senate, the republican counterpart of the old council of kings of the tribal period. The senators enjoyed special privileges of precedence at public functions, wore special dress, and claimed for themselves exclusive occupancy of the main executive offices of the republic: the offices of consul and censor and the priesthoods of the state religion. Tradition had it that the Senate was composed of the heads of the one hundred most noble families, but historians generally believe that the early membership must have numbered around three hundred. By the end of the fifth century B.C., there were some senators of obviously plebeian origin, but they were differentiated from those of more ancient noble lineage. Most of the power was vested in the hands of the heads of the ancient families. These appointed the magistrates, invested them with the *imperium* (see below, pp. 93–94), debated all issues of public concern, dominated the law courts, and directed matters of foreign policy, war, and peace.

The patrician claim to exclusive control of Rome's political destiny was challenged by the plebeians, the non-noble citizens who worked the land and formed the backbone of the Roman army. One of the more interesting facts about early Roman history is that the common people appear from the very first as a fully class-conscious and highly organized political pressure group. They were jealous of their status as citizens and intent on making their voice heard in the determination of civic affairs. They were poorer than their patrician counterparts, and the economic depression that followed upon Rome's severance of relations with the Etruscans threatened many with bankruptcy and a fall into slavery for failure to pay their debts. This led to an intensification of class conflict and a struggle that ultimately resulted in the plebeians' rights as citizens of the republic.

Originally the plebeians voiced their discontent in the tribal assembly, the *Comitia curiata*, a meeting of the entire Roman citizenry, not by class, but by clans. The assembly had the right of confirming the appointments of magistrates made by the Senate, and it provided a forum in which the plebs could legally oppose the nobles and sue for reforms. Moreover, the plebs created their own counterpart to the Senate, the *Concilium plebis tributum*, or Assembly of the Plebeians by Tribes, in which they elected a spokesman (the tribune) to represent their cause to the Senate.

When the patricians refused to accede to their demands for political and economic reforms, the plebeians used a special tactic to force concessions. Since Rome was surrounded by hostile neighbors, the Roman army, made up of citizen-soldiers, was the mainstay, not only of Roman independence in general, but also of the safety of the patricians' lands. Therefore, instead of taking to arms and fomenting a civil war, the plebs merely threatened to secede from the republic unless their demands were met. In short, the plebs used nonviolent resistance against the upper class. And their resistance was effective because, without the plebeians, the Roman army could not exist.

The plebeians' resistance to exploitation by the patricians resulted ultimately in the delegation of political power to a new body, the *Comitia centuriata*, the Assembly of the Roman People by Military Units, which by the middle of the fifth century B.C. was enacting laws, electing magistrates, and exercising all of the powers formerly claimed by the Senate. The creation of this body did not mean that the Senate ceased to function; it still provided the leadership of the republic and provided the men to fill the main executive posts. But the freedom and political power of the plebeian class was assured for the time being, and the Romans now possessed a legislative body for effecting political reforms, when they were necessary, without resorting to revolution or civil war.

It is probable that the *Comitia centuriata* was responsible for enactment of Rome's first written law code, the Law of the Twelve Tables (451–450 B.C.). This code was not a revolutionary document; it sought to secure certain rights and privileges to both classes involved in the civil struggles of the first decades of independence. For example, it prohibited marriage between the classes, thus seeming to assure the "purity" of the aristocratic caste. More importantly, it guaranteed the right of life and liberty to the ordinary citizen. It allowed the common man to seek relief from his debts without being reduced to slavery. And it gave the right of appeal to the *Comitia curiata* to any citizen who felt that injustice had been done to him. In sum, very early on, the Roman commonwealth worked out a system of collective bargaining between the classes. It set up a kind of check-and-balance system in government, which permitted changes in the political structure of the commonwealth when such changes appeared desirable, but it discouraged rule by force alone, whether by class or individual.

THE IDEA OF ROMAN UNITY

All of this was consonant with the way the Romans conceived authority and power. According to Roman tradition, authority (*auctoritas*) derived from the will of the *entire* Roman people. But the Romans distinguished between the *authority* of the group and the *power* that that authority might confer on a given individual or magistracy. The power to wield political authority they designated by the term *imperium* (from which derive the English words imperial, imperious, and the like). *Imperium* was the power granted to a magistrate to act in certain matters in the interest of the whole people. No distinction was made between political, military, and judicial power; every public office was invested with *imperium*, and every duly elected magistrate exercised the *imperium* if the *auctoritas*, the moral authority of the people, stood behind his office. When a man acted on his own in public affairs, without the sustaining moral authority of the group, in leading a revolution or a military coup, he was said to be exercising *mere* force (*vis*), not *imperium*.

Thus the Romans distinguished between properly and improperly sanctioned political actions. A proper political action was one authorized by the Roman people, in the interests of the Roman people, and for the Roman people. It was assumed that, given the nature of the world, properly authorized actions would inevitably result in success. Conversely, of course, it was assumed that any action that was unsuccessful must have been either unauthorized or improperly authorized; for if an action were undertaken in the best interests of the group and under the proper religious auspices, it had to succeed. This kind of argument made success its own justification, which may account for

the famous "pragmatism" of the Romans in spite of their
equally legendary "conservative" nature.

The Romans were conservative in their reluctance to
launch any new project that deviated from the pattern of
behavior handed down from their past in traditions. But
if a man presumed to act on his own, carried out his action
successfully, and imposed his will upon the people, the
Romans were willing to concede that he might really have
possessed the *imperium* after all, or that he had understood the true nature of *auctoritas* better than the group.
For example, in theory the Romans manifested an abiding
fear of revolutions; but in fact they were willing to interpret a successful revolution as a manifestation of the sub-
conscious wisdom of the group. In the final analysis, only
unsuccessful revolutions horrified the Romans; for the failure of a rebellion indicated the presence of someone in their
midst who was insensitive to the moral excellence that had
allowed the Romans to survive and to prevail over their
enemies.

Auctoritas was not only present in the entire group
of living Roman citizens, it was present in the dead as well.
Traditional Roman religion taught that the dead lingered
on in their tombs as spirits requiring regular worship and
sacrifice by the family to which they had belonged, to keep
them from roaming the earth as ghosts and doing harm to
men. This belief reflected the Romans' profound sense of
their obligation to the past. The Roman populace was conceived to be continuous throughout time: the living, the
dead, and the as-yet-unborn were parts of a single ongoing
line; the past could make demands on the living, and the
living had to bear in mind their obligations to future generations. Above all, the living had to keep alive the moral
power that the ancestors had manifested in their achievements. Thus, *auctoritas* was quintessentially conservative; it

reinforced traditional behavior and undermined any rash
impulse to deviate from customs that had shown their virtue in past difficulties.

The *imperium* was another matter. The *imperium*
was the dynamic and innovative element in Roman life, as
auctoritas was the stabilizing and conservative element. The
right of exercising the *imperium* was claimed as a sole pre-
rogative of the patriciate in the early days of the Republic.
The Law of the Twelve Tables, however, secured to the
lower class their right to share in the expression of *auctoritas*. And it was only a matter of time before the plebs
claimed the right to exercise the *imperium* as well. When
the plebs secured admission to offices invested with the *imperium*, they assured the unity of the Roman people. They
also opened the way to the creation of a new nobility, a nobility of talent rather than of birth.

The wars that Rome fought with its neighbors in
the early fourth century B.C. decimated the patrician class
and enriched certain of the plebeian families by extending
their landholdings. But while the old prohibition against
intermarriage between the classes was observed, the older
families had no way of strengthening or even sustaining
their lines. The result was that more and more of the executive offices had to be opened up to talented plebeians. By the
end of the fourth century B.C., all of the offices formerly
claimed as the exclusive preserve of the patricians were
held by men of plebeian origins. The patrician class sought
to save their privileged position by inducting anyone who
held the office of consul into the Senate. This expedient was
only partly successful, however; it really resulted in the
creation of two aristocracies, one descended from the ancient
and increasingly weak nobility, and another of talented new
men who were in but not of the "true" nobility.

In the early third century B.C. the situation was regu-

larized by reforms that purged the Senate of anyone
deemed unworthy to exercise its august authority. Membership in the Senate was now redistributed by the censors on
the basis of landed wealth. Political power was in effect
handed over to those whose ownership of land would presumably instill in them a proper interest in the well-being of the commonwealth. But the distinction between patrician and plebeian was maintained. The new plutocratic
aristocracy assumed the privileges and style of life of the
older nobility; and during the wars with Carthage in the
third century, it became in effect a new hereditary ruling
caste. During those wars it also became fantastically rich,
self-centered, and greedy. In fact, it soon manifested the attitudes of the old aristocracy that it had displaced, by at-
tempting to exclude the common people from the enjoyment
of the material benefits the empire might afford them. This
caused a new period of civil strife in Rome, which, this
time, was not characterized by nonviolent resistance on the
part of the common people. By the middle of the second century B.C., the Roman plebs had been reduced to poverty and
political deprivation in the midst of a material plenty never
before even contemplated in Rome. And just when Rome began to emerge as peacemaker of the world abroad, it entered into a cycle of civil wars at home that threatened to
destroy not only Rome, but other higher civilizations of the
Mediterranean basin as well.

The Era of Civil Wars: 133-31 B.C.

The acquisition of an empire had profoundly dis-
turbing effects on the social order and administrative structure of the Roman Republic. The Punic, Macedonian, and

Syrian Wars had kept the Roman soldiery far from Italy for many years. The campaigns in the East brought the Roman peasant-soldiers into contact with "softer" nations and gave them a taste for luxuries that the simple farm life at home could never provide. Often the soldiery developed a greater loyalty to the land in which they were serving than to Rome itself. The foreign wars also transformed the Roman army from a citizen militia into a *professional* fighting force. Many of the Roman legionnaires were not interested in returning to Italy when their terms of military service ended. They had become used to the spoils of victory, and often they were more devoted to their commanders than to the agents sent with instructions from that distant body of "civilians" in the Senate at home.

At the same time, the enormous wealth that Rome's conquests abroad had channeled into the home market became concentrated in the hands of the senatorial class. The patricians used this wealth to buy out small landowners and to create great plantations (*latifundia*). There was little work for the bankrupt peasants on these plantations, because the patricians found it cheaper to use the vast number of slaves that the foreign wars had made available. The small farmers who did manage to survive found it difficult to compete on the local market. Not only did the plantation owners flood the market with their produce, the market itself was consistently depressed by the flow of grain products from Sicily and North Africa.

The peasants were, as a result, progressively driven off the land and into the cities. There they lived on the dole paid by the state out of the profits of empire, became hangers-on of noble patrons, or made a living by selling their votes to the ward heelers of the growing number of political machines. Those who did not care to live such an inse-

cure existence went into the army, to swell the ranks of
professionals who lived by their fighting ability alone and
who pursued war, not in defense of the fatherland, but as a
profit-making venture. The restless urban masses thus created were a potential source of revolutionary disturbance in
the later days of the republic. And so were the professional
soldiers who increasingly demanded a fair share of the
fruits of empire won by their labor and blood.

Thus, soon after the end of the Punic Wars, Roman
politics became characterized by a threefold competition for
the wealth created by the empire. The senatorial class
wanted to maintain its privileged position in Roman imperial political and economic life. The urban masses were generally disaffected, and their disaffection could be mobilized
by demagogues and political adventurers, of either lower-
class or patrician origins, who wanted to enrich themselves
at the expense of the senatorial monopoly. The army, which
had come to constitute a third force in Roman politics,
was increasingly disgusted by the narrowness of the senatorial class and the apparent greed and instability of the
masses. As the situation degenerated, the army assumed
an increasingly important role in Roman politics as mediator, judge, and court of appeal for both classes.

THE GRACCHI, MARIUS, AND SULLA:
133–78 B.C.

By 133 B.C., Roman civic politics had polarized
around two factions. One party called itself the Optimates
—that is, the better people—and represented the interests
of the wealthiest families of the senatorial class. The Optimates presented themselves as defenders of the "good old

ways" of Roman tradition. The other faction was known as the Populares—champions of the depressed segment of the citizenry. It demanded the redistribution of the land, reform of voting procedures, and revision of the system by which the empire was administered and its benefits were distributed. The struggle between these two factions degenerated into civil war when the Senate, having grown fearful of the power of a popularist leader, Tiberius Gracchus, resorted to assassination to rid itself of its opposition.

Tiberius Gracchus had been elected tribune in 133 B.C. It was his plan to repossess the public lands of Rome, to subdivide them into individual holdings, and to settle the Roman citizenry on them with funds adequate to assure their continued independence. His assassination by members of the senatorial party cut short the execution of his plans, but his younger brother, Gaius Gracchus, elected tribune in 123 B.C., took them up once more. Gaius's aims were even more revolutionary than those of his brother, encompassing nothing less than the transformation of Rome into a democracy along classical Greek lines. The Senate responded to this challenge by declaring martial law, which caused a series of bloody riots, in which Gaius and some three thousand members of the Popular party were killed.

The attention of both parties was temporarily distracted from civic affairs by slave rebellions at home, invasions of northern Italy by German tribesmen, and the defection of allies in North Africa. In the end, however, these "distractions" only pointed up the weaknesses of senatorial government; for the armies sent by the Senate to deal with the situation were badly officered, unwilling to fight, and often corrupt in the extreme.

The situation was saved by Gaius Marius (157–86 B.C.), a brilliant soldier of lower-class origin, who raised a professional fighting force on his own and accomplished what neither the Senate nor the regular army had been able to do. Marius was victorious in both North Africa (107–105) and northern Italy (102–101); he reformed the army; and in a series of consulships, he tried to carry through some of the reforms envisioned by the Gracchi. As virtual dictator, his power resting on the loyalty of his personal army, Marius was the prototype of the kind of politician that would dominate Roman politics for the next century. Even his downfall came about in what was to become the usual way with his successors—that is, through the rise of another adventurer even more talented and more politically astute than he was.

Marius's lieutenant, Lucius Cornelius Sulla (138–78 B.C.), played on the Senate's fear of Marius to win for himself a command in the East, with which he both enriched himself and created an army especially loyal to him. On his return from the East in 83 B.C., he wiped out the remnants of Marius's party, exiled Marius's sympathizers, had himself proclaimed dictator for life in 81 B.C., and ruled as virtual king until his death in 78 B.C.

The careers of Marius and Sulla represent the path to political power in first-century Rome. The stages of this path were, first, senatorial fear of the lower classes and the lower classes' resentment of senatorial privileges, followed by the appearance of a talented soldier-hero willing to play off one class against another in order to win a great command, his use of the great command to create a personal army, and, finally, his march on Rome at the head of this army to bring "peace and prosperity" to the populace. Such was the pattern followed by Pompey in the 60s, by Crassus in the 50s, and by Julius Caesar in the 40s. It was the pattern that Mark Antony tried to follow in the 30s, but he failed. For he was opposed by an astute politician—Octavian—who recognized that permanent power and stability would come only through a breaking of the pattern that had prevailed up to his time.

POMPEY, CRASSUS, AND JULIUS CAESAR: 78–44 B.C.

The death of Sulla was followed by another series of crises, both at home and abroad. Again there were slave rebellions, such as that led by Spartacus in 73–71 B.C. Rome's allies in Italy rose, some demanding the status of citizens, others demanding their freedom from Rome; pirates in the Mediterranean formed what were in effect independent principalities; and there were further mutinies among the legions. Out of this turmoil two new political leaders appeared, Pompey (Gnaeus Pompeius, 106–48 B.C.), and Marcus Licinius Crassus (112–53 B.C.). Pompey and Crassus combined military talent and wealth, and in 70 B.C. they held the consulship together. They brought temporary peace to Italy and stability, for a while, to the Mediterranean, but at a price: both hungered for the kind of total power that Sulla had enjoyed during his dictatorship. But in their entourage there was another political adventurer who would eventually emerge victorious over both of them, Julius Caesar (100–44 B.C.).

When Pompey went to Asia Minor to put down the long-lived rebellion of the Pontic king Mithridates VI, Crassus and Caesar conspired against him. This drove Pompey into alliance with the senatorial party, now led by Marcus Tullius Cicero (106–43 B.C.). But when, upon his return from the East, Pompey asked the Senate to reward the troops that had served both him and the Senate so well, the Senate foolishly refused. This led Pompey to seek another alliance with Crassus and Caesar. In 60 B.C. these three formed the First Triumvirate and effectively split up the entire Roman world between them. Pompey remained in Rome and controlled Spain, Crassus took command of the eastern provinces, and Caesar was given Gaul.

Caesar remained in Gaul from 58 to 50 B.C., where he built up his reputation as a soldier and patriot, amassed a fortune with which to buy votes and allies, and created an army that was fanatically devoted to him alone. When Crassus was killed in the East in 53 B.C., in a campaign against the Parthians that had been meant to give him a military reputation to complement his vast wealth, the leaders of the senatorial party again made successful overtures to Pompey. Therefore, when Caesar returned to Italy from Gaul he was faced by a combined force of Pompey's veterans and the senatorial army. But Pompey fell before Caesar's troops at Pharsalus, in Greece, in 48 B.C., and the senatorial armies sustained defeats in Asia, Africa, and Spain.

By 46 B.C., Caesar was sole ruler of the Roman world. He seemed to have no overall program for the regeneration of Rome, although he did identify himself with the Popular party and undertook a number of reforms calculated to relieve the plight of the poor. Unlike Sulla, he did not take revenge upon the senatorial opposition; on the contrary, he tried to reach a *modus vivendi* with it, for he needed it to administer the empire of which he meant, apparently, to make himself king after the model of Alexander. The Senate remained recalcitrant, however, and on the eve of Caesar's departure for Asia, where he intended to secure the frontiers against the Parthians, a group of senatorial conspirators, led by Cassius and Brutus, struck him down.

MARK ANTONY AND OCTAVIAN

After having committed the deed, however, the Senatorial party was gripped by irresolution. Caesar's soldiers and the Roman mob rose in protest; Caesar's lieutenant Mark Antony (82–30 B.C.) seized Caesar's mantle and undertook a systematic elimination of the senatorial party. The massacre was stopped only when Caesar's will was opened and it was discovered that not Mark Antony, but Caesar's twenty-one-year-old nephew Gaius Julius Caesar Octavianus was the late dictator's heir. For a while, it seemed as if another war, between Antony and Octavian, must ensue; but Caesar's army insisted on their alliance against the murderers of Caesar, and in 43 B.C. the Second Triumvirate was formed, made up of Antony, Octavian, and the consul Lepidus, a friend of Caesar's.

Again the empire was split up among the three rulers. Mark Antony took the eastern provinces as his personal preserve; Octavian remained in control of the West; and Lepidus was consigned to Sicily and North Africa. Antony left friends and allies behind in Rome, but these gradually abandoned him as he fell under the charms of the East. Antony's alliance with Cleopatra allowed Octavian to suggest that Antony contemplated the creation of a separate empire. It also allowed Octavian to present Antony as the enemy of all that was truly Roman and Caesarian in spirit. By clever diplomacy and propaganda, Octavian effected an alliance with the remnants of the senatorial party, eliminated Lepidus, and offered himself as the sole possible restorer of the "good old Roman ways."

Octavian possessed three advantages in his contest with Antony. He commanded enormous wealth, inherited from Caesar; he had Caesar's name; and he was supported by the ablest general of the empire, Marcus Agrippa (63–12

B.C.), who apparently aspired to no political power for himself. Octavian offered himself as the heir of *both* Caesar and the Senate. When the break with Antony finally came, Octavian held all the cards.

By the time Octavian broke with Antony, the Roman populace was tired: it had endured over a century of civil strife, and it wanted peace. It wanted to enjoy the fruits of empire; it was offended by Antony's apparent defection to the East; and it rallied, aristocrat and pleb, to Octavian's standard. At the battle of Actium in 31 B.C., the forces of Antony and Cleopatra were defeated.

The Augustan Age

Octavian was now in full control of the situation. He appeared as the savior of his country against the Eastern peril; and he seemed to be the one man capable of healing the wounds of civil war. He obliged everyone by rising to the occasion, not least by living to a ripe old age. He ruled Rome from 31 B.C. to A.D. 14, which gave him time enough to identify himself with the fortunes of Rome in the imaginations of the Senate, the people, and the army. His reforms, the manner in which he presented them, and his longevity contributed to the notion that he was more than human, a hero certainly, and possibly even a god. Here at last, it seemed, was the redeemer whom the peoples of the Mediterranean had long been awaiting.

THE AUGUSTAN REFORMATION
OF THE EMPIRE

In 27 B.C. Octavian took the name Augustus, a name religious in its connotations. The governmental system that he worked out for the empire was a masterpiece of com-

promise between inherited traditions and the exigencies of
the current social, political, and economic reality. That system saved the empire; but in the long run it dealt the death
blow to republican institutions. Augustus did not do away
with those institutions; he merely united all its offices in
his own person. There was no necessity of having himself
proclaimed king; the various offices of the republic so united
offered more than enough power for any man. He was at
once consul, tribune, chief priest of the civic religion, and
censor. Above all, Augustus ruled by personal prestige: he
was *princeps* (first citizen) and *pater patriae* (father of
his country). In his personal life he tried to incarnate the
ideals of civic virtue and responsibility, which had been
lacking for so long among patricians and plebeians alike.

Basically, Augustus faced a fourfold problem. Most
important was the security of the frontiers, which, because
of the armies' involvement in the civil wars, had disintegrated. The army itself constituted another problem; it had
grown to unmanageable size and formed what was in effect
a state within a state. Third, the city proletariat and the
small farmer had to be taken care of. And, fourthly, the
new regime had to promote goodwill and confidence among
the senatorial class if a viable administrative system was
to be set up.

Augustus's reform of the provincial administration
system struck at all of these problems. First, the frontiers
were consolidated, and it became a matter of public policy
not to extend the boundaries of empire any further. This
allowed reduction of the size of the army, which was now
placed under sole command of the *princeps* and stationed
mainly in the frontier provinces, where it could protect
the citizenry and yet remain removed from the temptation
to meddle in Roman civic affairs. A special corps, the Praetorian Guard, charged with defending the life of the *prin-*

ceps, was stationed near Rome. The interior provinces, which required no army to protect them but only a police force, Augustus entrusted to the rule of the senatorial class, thus assuring their allegiance to his regime. The governors of these provinces were chosen exclusively from the senatorial aristocracy, which allowed it to appear as if the Senate were still a vital force in the life of the empire and thus salved patrician pride. Finally, a special fund was set up for the *princeps* to use as he saw fit, and a special administrative corps was established. The new imperial bureaucracy was chosen from the order of "knights," a class of wealthy men who did not enjoy senatorial rank but who nonetheless constituted a major source of administrative talent by virtue of their background in commerce. The province of Egypt was made the personal preserve of the *princeps*, out of which he could provide the grain dole for the indigent Roman populace.

These reforms promoted increased flexibility in the society and temporarily stabilized the economy. The Mediterranean basin became a self-sufficient economic unit, although the western half of the empire remained primarily agrarian, while the eastern half continued to be a center of manufacturing and commerce.

There were, however, certain flaws in the system that were not readily discernible in Augustus's own time. The system was a complex of mutually interdependent areas of production and consumption, which meant that the loss or failure of any one of them could hurt the whole. Another flaw was that the whole system rested on slave labor. With the consolidation of the frontiers and the resulting peace, the supply of new slaves was gradually reduced. Over the years many slave families succeeded in winning their freedom and attained to citizen status, with the result that the manpower required to maintain the great estates was gradually drained off the farms. The western cities grew, but they were essentially consumers, not producers, and whether the economy waxed or waned, the city-dwellers insisted on being taken care of as the Roman populace was. Finally, since the eastern half of the empire was primarily productive of commercial goods, while the western half was productive of agricultural products, the balance of trade and wealth always tended to favor the East.

Thus two kinds of divisions among the citizens of the empire were possible: between city-dwellers and farm-dwellers on the one hand and between the eastern provinces and the western provinces on the other. In the civil wars, which broke out in 68 A.D. and again in the third century AD., the parties tended to divide along these lines. For all its size and complexity, the Roman Empire was a delicately balanced mechanism resting on the backs of slaves and depending ultimately on the good will of the army charged with the task of defending it against its enemies, foreign and domestic. The absence of truly dangerous external enemies for nearly two centuries did not test rigorously the soundness of the system or the claim of the empire to provide political stability to eternity. The vast reserves of money, manpower, and land accumulated during the period of expansion saw the Romans through most of the crises that threatened them up to the third century. For two centuries, therefore, the Augustan system worked well. It provided the material and political base of a cultural achievement comparable in its depth and range to that of the Greeks of the Periclean Age. And it produced a society from which a wide enough range of satisfactions could be had to allow a modern admirer of it to call it the happiest time in the history of mankind.

THE TRANSFORMATION OF ROMAN CULTURE
IN THE LATE REPUBLICAN AGE

Augustus's reforms were not limited to political, economic, and social matters. They also envisaged a fundamental reorientation of Roman culture. Augustus tried to purge the Romans of the last vestiges of their primitive ethnocentrism. He turned the city of Rome into a world capital, and he taught the Romans to identify their own destiny with that of mankind at large. He convinced them that they had been especially chosen to bring peace and security to the world. And he gave them pride in the task of imperial administration, which they had tended to consider up to that time as either a burden or merely an opportunity for personal enrichment. By the end of Augustus's reign, the Roman Empire had been changed into a genuine cosmopolis. The Greeks had thought primarily in terms of the world of the city; the Romans under Augustus came to think of the entire world as a city, in which every man might, in time, enjoy the rights of a citizen.

Roman tradition offered unique possibilities for the kind of spiritual reform envisaged by Augustus. The Romans had always regarded *piety* as the supreme religious value and *discipline* as the prime civic virtue. Unlike the Greeks, they had never thought that the good life was possible *only* within the confines of their native city. According to Roman belief, one's human qualities could be cultivated anywhere—on the deserts of Africa, in the forests of Germany, on the plains of Hungary; in teeming cities and in the quiet of a rural retreat; in one's relations with one's friends, relatives, and fellow citizens; in contests with one's enemies or with raw nature; as a soldier, a farmer, a lawyer, a philosopher, or a politician. But they did not believe that the cultivation of one's humanity was an end in itself. On the contrary, they held that one's humanity was manifested in the way one discriminated between different kinds of duties and the way one gave to each of his various roles its due weight and attention.

They did not see their various public and private roles as necessarily conflicting. Again, unlike the Greeks, the Romans continued to believe, until very late in their history, in the providential nature of the world-process. The world, they believed, was governed by an essential order and harmony; and anyone could share in that order and harmony if he remained pious and disciplined. Personal self-development and public duties were complementary sides of the total world-process. The height of wisdom was to know one's duty and to do it, not to pursue narrow self-interest or to yield to immediate pleasures. In short, the Romans were natural Stoics. And the greatest Stoic of them all, Cato the Elder (234–149 B.C.), opposed the introduction of Greek cultural ideals into Roman life because he believed that Rome could learn nothing new from the Greek Stoics and could only suffer from exposure to Greek Epicureanism. To later Romans, Cato became a symbol of all that had been plain, honest, and vigorous in republican times. A pleb by origin, he had enjoyed a brilliant career as soldier, orator, administrator, lawyer, and politician. When serving as censor in 184 B.C., he had ruthlessly purged Rome of Hellenistic practices and inaugurated a "puritan" reaction against the luxury and idleness of the upper classes.

He had also been fearful of the effects of imperial expansion on the good old Roman ways, although he profited from it as much as others of his class. He therefore tried, in vain, to keep Rome rural and simple in an age of growing complexity, wealth, and cosmopolitanism. In his

personal manner, he consistently affected the role of the
simple farmer—plain-spoken, canny, unyielding in his con-
tempt for softness in any form. His conception of the "true"
Roman values was set forth in his speeches to the Senate,
his tract *On Farming* (which was as much a moral as a
technical treatise), and his history of Rome. In the first century B.C., therefore, Cato's ideas provided a moral ground
for the reactionary ideas of the senatorial class. Brutus and
Cato the Younger, for example, invoked his name as the
antithesis of everything for which Julius Caesar stood.

But the austere philosophy of Cato represented an
age that was passing rather than a portent of things to
come. Two forces worked against full adoption of his ideas
in the age inaugurated by Augustus: the luxury of the upper classes and the popularity of those Greek ideals that
Cato had opposed.

During Cato's own lifetime, Greece had become a
fashionable educational center for Roman society. The Roman upper classes sent their sons to Greece for schooling;
educated Romans wrote in Greek; Greek slaves served as
nursemaids and tutors of Roman youths. Ironically, the ultimate destroyer of Cato's nemesis, Carthage, was Scipio
Africanus the Younger (185–129 B.C.), patron of a brilliant
literary circle in which Greek cultural values predominated.
And it was a Greek, Polybius of Megalopolis (205–120 B.C.),
who finally taught the Romans to see their own national
history—as Cato had written it—within the context of a
universal civilization more Greek than Roman. Polybius
was a friend of Scipio the Younger, and he represented the
prestige that Greek thought and manners increasingly enjoyed in the once tradition-ridden and ethnocentric Roman
aristocracy. Roman philhellenism found expression during
the next century in the lyric poetry of Catullus (84–54 B.C.),
the didactic poetry of Lucretius (98–54 B.C.), the historiog-

raphy of Sallust (86–34 B.C.), and the philosophical thought of Cicero (106–43 B.C.).

Lucretius may be taken as representative of the attempt to import Greek ideas in undiluted form to Rome. Having grown up during the era of civil wars, Lucretius was acutely sensitive to the need for a new theoretical substructure for the changed life-style of the Roman people. He found the theory he needed in the thought of the Greek philosopher Epicurus (341–271 B.C.); in his poem *On the Nature of Things*, Lucretius expounded a thoroughgoing materialism as the sole possible basis for a distinctively human life. His poem is a hymn to reason as the best instrument for perceiving the true nature of reality and for promoting the kind of freedom in which true pleasure is heightened and pain diminished.

The world, Lucretius held, was nothing but the product of random atomic combination. It followed, therefore, that all intrinsic meaning or purpose—on the basis of which an absolute morality could be prescribed—had to be denied. Religion was the product of ignorance and any thought of life after death a delusion. Not even tradition could be honored in Lucretius's world, for tradition itself was the product of superstition, fear of the future, inability to see the truth. Enlightened self-interest must serve as the basis for both individual and social development, Lucretius maintained.

In his political philosophy, Lucretius taught that the state was a mere expedient; there was nothing sacred about it. It followed, therefore, that the individual should give his loyalty to the state only as long as his own self-interest was being served. And this implied that when one ceased to benefit from participation in a given society, he was justified in withdrawing from it.

The individual's sole responsibility was to himself.

Since man had but one life, a life without intrinsic meaning, it followed that one's purpose was to increase the pleasure offered in the time given him. Like Epicurus, Lucretius conceived pleasure primarily in intellectualist rather than in physical terms. Pleasure was relief from the pain inevitably caused by those random, purposeless, and ineluctable changes in the world process. To liberate oneself from false expectations in a world governed by chance was the best men could hope for. Thus, salvation, to Lucretius, was essentially intellectual; it was given only to those who recognized the absurdity of all striving.

But in the chaotic Roman world of the first century B.C., the Epicurean doctrine of pleasure-seeking could easily be interpreted as a mandate to serve oneself in cruder ways. The Lucretian attitude appeared in a more sensual form in the erotic poetry of Catullus, who instructed his readers to "consume the days" in the pursuit of bodily pleasure. It also appeared in the historical works of Sallust, a follower of Julius Caesar, who saw the pursuit of the main chance as the only rule governing relations between man and man.

Julius Caesar himself may be taken as an enlightened Epicurean in politics: his personal demeanor and public opportunism were sustained by a materialism as radical as anything imagined by Lucretius. Caesar's disregard for conventional morality, for political tradition, and for religious custom was, perhaps, the main reason for his failure to convince the Senate that his program was constructive.

Augustus apparently profited from reflection on Caesar's fate in a way that Mark Antony did not. Augustus's manner suggested a proper blending of Roman traditionalism and Greek rationalism. In fact, Augustus's conception of the role of the *princeps* in Roman society approximates very closely the ideal of leadership set forth by Caesar's political enemy, Cicero, who was also Lucretius's enemy in philosophy.

Cicero lived during the period of civil war, and in the end he died in defense of the Catonian ideal. A newcomer to the senatorial ranks, he had the kind of passion for tradition that is not uncommon among newly arrived men in a hierarchical society. Yet he was by no means a narrow-minded ideologue. He idolized Greek thought, especially in its Platonic and Stoic forms, but he was open to the necessity of reform from time to time in even the best-founded society. To him the Epicurean attitude was reprehensible, not only because of its lack of reverence for society, but because it failed to comprehend what he considered the true nature of human reason.

Cicero did not conceive human reason as standing over against religion, as Lucretius did, but as complementing it, illuminating it, and turning it to civilizing uses. For him, human reason was less an instrument for gratifying basic animal needs than an expression in man of that ordering principle that underlay the entire world-process. Unlike Lucretius, who saw man as naturally animalistic, Cicero viewed natural man as containing within him potentialities for growth and development that found their proper outlet and realization only in society. In society, Cicero held, man finally transcended primitive animal needs and attained to peculiarly human forms of expression: piety, a sense of duty, and self-discipline. Thus, just as reason complemented religion, so society complemented nature. And within society itself, public obligations attained a balance with private needs, to create an area in which man could attempt to realize the good life under conditions of security and plenty. To maintain and extend self-consciously the orderly and harmonious balance of private and public needs, Cicero held, was the true function of the state. Therefore, the state was no mere expedient, to be served or abandoned as immediate self-interest demanded, but the capstone of world-reason itself.

In Cicero's view, the Roman republic was especially blessed by nature because in it the task of balancing private and public needs had been embraced as a living ideal from the beginning. Rome had managed, therefore, to avoid the extremes of monarchical autocracy on the one hand and democratic anarchy on the other throughout her long history. In Rome, the state had emerged as the custodian and guarantor of a legal tradition that stressed discussion and compromise rather than strife and party dissension. Above all, the Roman state had consistently secured the institution of private property, without which the individual was inevitably exposed to the vagaries of arbitrary public power.

The republican form of government was ideal, in Cicero's view, because it allowed the broadest possibilities for compromise and adjustment between the various needs and desires of the total citizenry. He recognized, however, that in times of stress and crisis, extraordinary measures might be needed to keep the governing classes from abandoning their responsibilities to the whole citizenry. And he entertained the notion of a kind of hero-savior, standing above parties, classes, and interest-groups, to whom total power might be given for a while to keep the state honest and the society intact. This hero-savior Cicero conceived in the image of Scipio the Younger, a man who combined the virtues of soldier, philosopher, and statesman in equal measure.

THE IDEALS OF THE AUGUSTAN AGE

Julius Caesar was too much the opportunist for Cicero's taste, and in the end Cicero opposed him. But the lesson of Julius Caesar's fall was not lost on Augustus. He seems to have wanted to present himself as the kind of hero-savior that Cicero had imagined in his Scipionic dream. At least, this is how Augustus's two most brilliant eulogists, the historian Livy (59 B.C.–A.D. 17) and the poet Virgil (70–19 B.C.) presented him in their great contributions to the Golden Age of Latin Literature.

Both Livy and Virgil wanted to show that Augustus incarnated a perfect balance of respect for tradition and realistic innovation, which, in their view, had characterized Roman history from its earliest times. Livy's history of Rome demonstrated how the destiny of any particular Roman was less significant than Roman destiny in general. According to him, Rome's success was not due to the talents of individual men or even of groups of men, but was derived from the very nature of the world. Virtue is given to individuals and to peoples at birth, and they show that virtue by their constancy in the face of temptation and adversity. Roman society is continuous with the nature from which it sprang; its virtue is incarnated in its institutions, customs, and conventions. Roman conservatism is therefore justified; it is a necessary barrier to the corroding effects of excessive individualism.

This did not mean that heroic assertion of all kinds is to be deplored. Quite the contrary, Livy suggests: anything that supports, defends, or renews Roman tradition is good. In short, creative action always consists in a *return* to the sacred ways of the fathers, as the career of Augustus showed, not in innovation. Reason was a tool, which had to be controlled and used for the maintenance of order in society, not used as a means of revising things. The state, then, is not an instrument of expression for an individual or any specific group; it is an expression of the world-process to which the masses must be encouraged to give unthinking allegiance. The era of civil wars that preceded the foundation of the Augustan principate evidenced the fall away from the virtuous traditions of the fathers; Augustus brought peace precisely because he had returned to the good old ways of the Romans. Augustus's very success was testimony to his adherence to the established order, that order of the world of which the earliest Romans were the perfect expression.

Virgil offered the poetic counterpart of Livy's great prose epic of Rome. He is the spokesman for the ideal of the *pax romana*, the Roman peace. Acutely sensitive to the special role that fate had singled out the Romans to play, he saw it as Rome's destiny to unify the known civilized world and to transform it into a cosmopolis. Like Livy, Virgil viewed Rome's triumph over all contenders as a function of an unchangeable *character*; but he gave to that character a *cosmopolitan* cast from the very first.

The *Aeneid* draws a picture of the Romans as a chosen people whose original home was in Asia, in Troy specifically. From Troy, Rome's forebears were led by the hero-founder, Aeneas, to Italy, where they merged with the Latins and Greeks. Thus ancient Rome was composed, by Virgil's account, of all the major stocks of the Mediterranean world: Trojan, Greek, and Latin. The subsequent evolution of the Roman people is conceived to be watched over by Venus, the goddess of love, who symbolizes the Roman husbandry of the land, the bounty of nature, and that respect for the natural forces of the universe that constitutes the basis of Roman civil life. Apollo, the god of light and reason, also looks with special favor on them, allowing them to foresee the future, to comprehend the true nature of the world-process, and to attain to a higher vision of justice for men than anything allowed to other peoples.

There is nothing tragic in Virgil's vision: everything is for the best in the best of all possible worlds. To accept one's task, to work and prosper in it, and to labor for the order of nature, on the land, in the family, and in the state, is the height of the good life. The reward for all this labor is a great world empire, cosmopolitan in principle, in which all men potentially have a place. In Augustus—Virgil suggests—that labor is consummated; he is an extraordinary man, but only in degree, not in kind. With his advent, history effectively comes to an end; the millennium arrives; the true meaning of life—a specifically Roman meaning—is revealed. Henceforth, Virgil seems to say, one need only perform his task as Rome defines it and the result will be a heaven on earth, a land of milk and honey, in which the lamb will lie down with the lion in eternal peace and prosperity. In this conviction Virgil reflected the gamble of Augustus himself, the gamble that men of good will, working together under selfless leadership, could provide a paradise on earth, which had been conceived only as a transcendental possibility by other peoples in the ancient world.

THE ACHIEVEMENT OF AUGUSTAN CULTURE

It is often said that Roman high culture was ultimately only a translation of Greek cultural values in terms of the needs of a cosmopolitan empire. There is some justification for this view, but it does not tell the whole story. In fact, it leaves unanswered a more basic question: How was it that the Romans succeeded in envisaging a *world* civilization in the first place?

The Romans did find in Greek culture much that was congenial to their own preconceptions about the world-process. And they found much that corresponded to what they intuitively took to be man's task on this earth. But Greek culture had been obsessed with the problem of *individual* self-cultivation; it did not advance a conception of society that transcended the narrowly circumscribed world of the *polis* and embraced the common interest of men everywhere. Roman civilization, however, was based on a faith in man's ability to provide the good life, not only for a small group of individuals provisionally united in mutual self-interest, but for a world polity composed of the most diverse elements and peoples. In this they were more like the Persians than the Greeks, and there may be some higher, poetic justice in Virgil's linking them to the Orient in his poem.

But there was another, distinctly non-Greek element in Roman culture: this was the overriding *optimism* that allowed the Romans to confront creatively the awful truths revealed in the tragic vision of life. If the Greeks ultimately came to rest in a Dionysiac conception of the true nature of the world, the Romans may be said to have remained obstinately Apollonian in their world-view. If the Greeks were sensitized to the chaos that lay at the root of life, the Romans were equally sensitized to the possibilities for creating order out of that chaos. The Greek tragic vision did reveal genuine truths about the nature of the world, of society, and of the gods, which, in an atmosphere of general success, tempered human pride with a commendable caution. But that same tragic vision could, in times of radical crisis, also act to undermine man's faith in his ability to act creatively in his own behalf. The truths of the Greek tragic vision were not totally lost on the Romans, but they were essentially a "comic" people; their experience and their inherited world-view made them much more sensitive to the *order* that lay exposed on the other side of the hero's tragic encounter with fate than the Greeks had ever been.

Finally, the Romans understood the advantages of role playing much better than the Greeks did. The Greeks played their roles on the stage and forgot that society itself requires a role-playing ability as great as that demanded of the actor. Augustus's last words are supposed to have been "Applaud, my friend; the comedy is finished." There was irony in the remark, but it was a kind of profound irony that allowed him to act *as if* order were possible, with such artistry as to make order a fact. The Roman innovation over the Greek social experience was contained in the conviction that a humanly contrived social order, *masquerading* as a function of the total world-process, could provide freedom and security simultaneously if it were extended to the entire world. Roman thinkers based their support of the Augustan experiment on the assumption that immediate successes or failures were less important than the long-range processes that govern the whole of human life. In the end, Cynics and Sceptics who predicted the fall of Rome were borne out; but not before the Romans had shown them the creative possibilities of secular optimism.

The Life and Death of Roman Imperial Civilization

The history of Rome from the reign of Augustus (31 B.C.–A.D. 14) to that of Constantine (A.D. 305–337) is the story of the gradual corrosion of the secular optimism fostered by the Augustan peace. It is a story that has often been dwelt upon as providing an object lesson in the perils of self-pride. At least, so Christian historians have regarded it, from St. Augustine to Toynbee. Less religiously inclined commentators have not been sure of what the story of the fall of the Roman Empire signifies. They have even found it difficult to agree on when the empire may be said to have finally expired. The great English historian Edward Gibbon, writing in the eighteenth century, felt compelled to bring the story of Rome's decline down to the conquest of Constantinople by the Turks in 1453. Most historians do not draw the story out so long; they are content to note certain weaknesses in the Augustan settlement and to trace their effects down to the time of Constantine in the early fourth century A.D.

Even though the city of Rome did not fall to the barbarians until the fifth century, there can be no doubt that the ultimate fate of the Roman state was sealed with its transformation into an oriental monarchy during the late third century A.D. When the emperor Constantine proclaimed Christianity the favored religion of the empire in 313 A.D., Rome had already become something radically different from what it had been under Augustus and his successors through the second century. Christianity was, in its own way, an optimistic religion, to be sure; it promoted a sense of public responsibility in its devotees from which the emperors could certainly profit. But Christianity was not secular in its aims; it directed men's attention to the other world and asked them to put off the pleasures of the earthly life in anticipation of a future heavenly reward. In this respect, Christianity opposed everything for which Greek and Roman humanism had stood.

This is not to say that the transformation of the Roman Empire into a Christianized oriental monarchy represented the "barbarization" that Gibbon took it to represent. At the time, it infused a new vitality into the languishing Roman social order. Moreover, it provided the sole possible bridge between the dying Roman world and the new cultures taking shape in northern Europe on the one hand and in Byzantium on the other. But the Christianization of the Roman Empire reflected the decision to abandon the classical attempt to build a specifically human world for all men on earth. Therefore, the triumph of Christianity in the empire can serve as a convenient terminal point for our account of the development of the Greco-Roman humanist tradition.

It is exceedingly difficult to convey anything of the magnificence of Roman imperial civilization in a short account. Ages of peace, prosperity, and stability are notoriously difficult to describe, in any event. Hegel once said that such ages are dull for the historian because it is only when men are suffering that they feel driven to record the facts of their lives. There is much truth in this. It is reflected in the absence of extensive documentation for the daily lives of men during the first two centuries of the Empire. It is confirmed by Gibbon's decision to begin his history, not with Augustus, but with the last of the emperors in the Augustan mold, Marcus Aurelius (d. A.D. 180). And it is shown in the conventional ordering of Roman imperial history, not in terms of its positive achievements, but in terms of its crises.

The principal crises of the imperial period were two: these may be called the crisis of leadership of A.D. 68–96 and the crisis of communal confidence of A.D. 235–285. The spacing of these two crises and their durations are significant. The first crisis was met successfully without requiring fundamental changes in the structure of the empire.

The second crisis required a total redefinition of imperial purpose and an overhaul of the entire society. The first was surmounted by drawing upon the legacy left by Augustus himself; the second constituted a repudiation of most of what Augustus had represented. The crisis of 68–96 resulted from the main flaw in Augustus's system: his failure to provide a mechanism of succession in the imperial office. But this crisis affected only the head of the social organism; it did not seriously endanger the body. The second crisis, that of 235–285, reflected a want of confidence in the imperial office per se. And from that crisis the imperial office emerged as a divine-right monarchy limited only by the moral suasion that the Christian religion could bring to bear upon it.

THE PROBLEM OF LEADERSHIP
AFTER AUGUSTUS

The Augustan settlement was a masterpiece of political compromise between old ideals and new realities; but like all compromises, it was ambiguous—and like all ambiguities, it raised as many problems as it solved. Above all, it confused the remnants of the older senatorial aristocracy. Was or was not the Senate responsible for the administration of the empire? Officially, the Senate possessed as much power as it had ever possessed; actually, it acted only at the pleasure of the *princeps*. If a senator showed too much initiative, he seemed to be challenging the power of the *princeps*; if he showed too little, he seemed to be uncooperative and ungrateful for what the *princeps* alone had been able to achieve. Wherein did the Senate's role actually lie? No one knew for sure. It took the subtlety of an Augustus to intuit "correct behavior" under the regime that he had inaugurated, and there was only one Augustus. During most of Augustus's rule, therefore, most senators contented themselves with the semblance of political power and the privileges that conformity to Augustus's will brought with it. Many senators nursed hopes of a time when things would return to the "good old ways" of the republic, but with very little enthusiasm and even less courage. The resentment that some members of the senatorial class nourished for Augustus never flamed into effective rebellion; it merely smoldered at the top of the political order of Rome, a source of debilitating second-guessing when the *princeps* erred in judgment, but no inspiration to creative opposition at all.

Augustus himself contributed to the sickness of the Senate while professing to be its physician. On the one hand, he claimed to be merely the first among equals—*princeps*, not *dominus* (lord)—and he pretended that he had no more *imperium* than any republican magistrate. On the other hand, he associated a number of talented individuals with him in ruling the empire, which suggested that he meant the principate to endure beyond his own lifetime. Then he confounded everybody by outliving one after another of his possible successors. Most of all, though, he confounded the man who actually did succeed him after all the other candidates had died, his talented soldier-stepson Tiberius (A.D. 14–37).

Tiberius was resentful of having remained unappreciated by Augustus, was suspicious of the Senate, and was uncertain of the loyalty of the army. During much of his reign he hid himself from public view, thereby adding to the mystery of the imperial office. Finally he gave vent to his (probably justified) sense of persecution by appointing the least-capable man in the Empire to succeed him as *princeps*. This was Gaius Caligula (37–41), a paranoid schizophrenic who was "classical" only in the perfection of his insanity. Caligula's insanity was manifested in a number of ways: in his megalomania, in his deification of himself and his sister, in his descent into the arena to participate in gladiatorial contests, and in his appointment of his horse to the Senate.

It is not known which of his insane actions touched off the palace rebellion that ultimately dispatched him; but when the furor died down, it was no senator, but the scholarly uncle of Caligula, Claudius (A.D. 41–54), who was installed by the Praetorian Guard while the Senate was still debating the restoration of the republic. Claudius showed a distinct talent for administration and an inclination to be an Augustan ruler in every way. But senatorial ire over the manner in which he had succeeded forced him into a permanent alliance with the army and rendered him susceptible to the influence of bureaucrats, courtiers, and—most dangerously—his wife, the notorious Agrippina II.

Agrippina prevailed upon Claudius to adopt her son Nero, who subsequently succeeded Claudius and ruled from A.D. 54 to 68. After a preliminary period of seemingly enlightened rule, Nero displayed the same characteristics as Caligula, with the sole difference that he provided accompaniment for his more aberrant crimes with music and poetry composed by himself. His arbitrary proscription of anyone who displeased him in the slightest way finally broke the patience of both the Senate and the army; in A.D. 68 the legions of Gaul, Spain, and Africa rose against him. Nero, in despair, committed suicide. And for a while the Senate had waved before it once more the possibility of a restored republic.

THE CRISIS OF LEADERSHIP: A.D. 68–96

The events of 68–69, however, quickly dispelled any hope of restoring the republic. From the provinces, one legion after another marched on Rome, with their commanders as candidates for the mantle of Nero. In the year 69 four different men actually made good their claims to imperial power. This was the "year of the four emperors"— Galba, Otho, Vitellius, and Vespasian, the first three of whom died violent deaths. Vespasian, formerly military commander and pacifier of Judea, a man of lower-class origins, restored order. He ruled from A.D. 69 to 79 and founded a new dynasty, the Flavian, which openly based imperial rule on the loyalty of the army and the purchased goodwill of the provincial nobility.

The rule of Augustus and his successors through Nero had been a military tyranny, in the last analysis; now the Flavians openly proclaimed the fact. According to Professor Michael Rostovtzeff, the empire had been transformed by Augustus into a kind of Hellenistic monarchy; that is to say, it was a confederation of cities linked together by commercial ties and held together by a military leader. Until the advent of Vespasian, however, the Roman populace had enjoyed a favored position in the empire, with privileges far in excess of those normally falling to a mere capital city. What the Flavians did, Rostovtzeff argues, was redress the balance of power between Rome and the provinces. Moreover, as Professor Max Carey has put it, Vespasian's succession showed that the imperial seat was no longer reserved for the nobility and that emperors could be made elsewhere than in Rome. Thus envisaged, the events of A.D. 68–69 may be viewed as revealing a kind of essential strength, rather than an essential weakness, in the empire. This strength had a twofold basis: the army and the economic wealth of the provinces. The Flavians recognized these sources of strength and acted accordingly. They took care to keep the army happy while disposing it in such a way as to remove from it any temptation to intervene arbitrarily in the political affairs of the empire. At the same time, the provincial nobility was given more control over local affairs, and the way was opened up for the advancement of provincials in the legions, in the imperial bureaucracy, and in the Senate itself.

The older Roman aristocracy was naturally resentful of Vespasian's policies; to them his reforms seemed to imperil the last vestiges of republican virtue and power. Vespasian was formally correct in his relations with the Senate, but it was obvious to all that he put the social and economic welfare of the whole empire above the narrow interests and claims of the Roman aristocracy. His reforms generated a new *esprit* in the legions and promoted a period of renewed economic growth in the provinces. The frontier defenses were strengthened—as in the upper Rhine, long a trouble spot—but no new expansion was undertaken. The Flavians were content, apparently, to grow fat from the profits accumulated by Augustus. Neither planters nor harvesters, the Flavians played the role of the cultivators of seedlings set out during the Augustan spring.

Vespasian's sons, Titus (79–81) and Domitian (81–96), continued his policies, although under Domitian the relations between the emperor and the Senate were strained to the breaking point. Domitian was much like Tiberius; he was secretive, sullen, suspicious, and resentful of the favor that his father had shown for his elder brother Titus. His implementation of his father's policies was carried forward with a vigor so excessive as to foster open resistance among certain factions of the Senate who now looked back nostalgically to republican times as an ideal age from which everything that had happened since was a decline. In A.D. 88 a rebellion in Germany, quickly suppressed, provided an excuse for the full release of Domitian's pent-up hatred of the old nobility. He instituted a reign of terror, marked by the rule of a secret police, arbitrary political assassination, proscription, and confiscation of the property of anyone even mildly suspected of anti-imperial sympathies. In the end, the Praetorian Guard intervened; with the aid of Domitian's wife, who was fearful for her own safety, the Guard finally murdered him. This time the Senate offered its own candidate for the imperial office, Nerva, whom the Guard saluted as emperor and who ruled from A.D. 96 to 98.

THE FIVE GOOD EMPERORS: A.D. 96–180

Nerva was no Augustus, but he tried to be. His rule was too short to allow him to carry out the moral and political reformation he envisaged; but it did allow him to institute a policy of imperial succession, which brought a much needed flexibility to the imperial office. Sensitive to the hostility of the army, which venerated all of the Flavians, including Domitian, Nerva placated the military by adopting as his son the talented general Trajan, associating him with his rule and designating him as his successor. This policy of adopting a talented soldier or administrator and associating him in the rule of the empire temporarily solved the problem of succession. Nerva's inauguration of this policy allowed him to be listed as one of the "five good emperors" who ruled in a spirit of Augustan efficiency, responsibility, and tolerance down to the death of Marcus Aurelius in 180.

All of the five good emperors were exceptional men,

but three of them were especially talented imperial admin-
istrators. These were Trajan (98–117), Hadrian (117–138),
and Antoninus Pius (138–161). Under them the frontiers
were consolidated in the north and in the east and their
defenses scientifically organized. Trajan fought extensive
wars in Dacia and Mesopotamia. These wars reflected the
beginning of new, and what would ultimately be disastrous,
pressures on the frontiers in those areas. But for the time
being, the barbarians were fended off, the frontiers held
firm, and the security of the Empire maintained. During this
period the emperors tightened their control over provincial
administration, but offices in the imperial bureaucracy were
progressively opened up to men of all classes; and agriculture, manufacturing, and commerce flourished. Public
building projects were undertaken throughout the empire,
and the cities took on the aspect of that style that we have
come to associate with imperial civilization everywhere
ever since.

Hadrian was an outstanding administrator. Building
on the popularity of Trajan's military successes, he made a
bid for senatorial support from the beginning. During his
twenty-one-year reign, he offered a model of enlightened
rule. He made many personal tours of inspection throughout
the length and breadth of the Roman world. His patronage
of the arts was prodigious. And his conservative military
policies, though unpopular with some, were beneficial to all.
His reign, however, with that of his successor Antoninus
Pius, betrays an air of autumnal satisfaction with past
achievement. It was a period of line-holding rather than innovation, and it was the calm before the storm that was
ultimately to wreck the empire. Barbarian pressures were
mounting on the frontiers; the decline of the supply of
slaves and the manumission of others had gravely weakened
the labor force on the great estates. Since the army was no

longer large enough to maintain the frontiers, it had become necessary to induct large numbers of barbarians into the auxiliary forces. As a result, Marcus Aurelius, the last of the five good emperors, had to spend most of his reign defending the frontiers. By the time he died, the frontiers were in turmoil, economic depression threatened most of the empire, and the imperial office itself had fallen into the hands of another madman, Marcus's own son, Commodus (180–192).

THE PROBLEM OF COMMUNAL CONFIDENCE
FROM COMMODUS TO DIOCLETIAN

Commodus represented a throwback to the type of Caligula and Nero. His belief that he was the incarnation of Hercules was only the most insane of his many obsessions. He was finally strangled by his own advisers, and was succeeded by Pertinax, a talented but unsuccessful reformer, who was in turn dispatched by the Praetorian Guard after a rule of only three months.

The imperial office now fell to a new kind of ruler, Septimius Severus (193–211), a kind of latter-day Marius who made no concessions to senatorial pride at all and based his power on the army alone. His first act upon entering Rome was to disband the Praetorian Guard, formerly recruited exclusively from the Roman and Italian citizenry, and open up membership in it to any Roman legionnaire. Severus then abandoned all pretense of being a mediator between the classes after the Augustan model. He filled the Senate with men of non-noble origins, tried to reform provincial administration even at the expense of the city of Rome, and bought off the Roman rabble with increased grain doles and circuses in the Coliseum.

Severus transformed the imperial office into a hereditary monarchy; as a result, his rule has often been portrayed as retrogressive. But he undertook consolidation of the frontiers, in Scotland and in the east. Furthermore, the Roman legal system was regularized during his rule, and its prescriptions were applied to everyone in the empire, without regard for class or place of birth. He had not learned from the mistake of Marcus Aurelius, however, and he left his son Caracalla (211–217) as his successor, with instructions to maintain peace at any price, reward the army, and ignore everything else. Like Commodus, Caracalla was slave to an obsession: he apparently believed that he was another Alexander the Great. While on a campaign in the Orient intended to prove that fact, he was assassinated. The same fate befell his successors, the pervert Heliogabalus (217–222) and the weakling Alexander Severus (222–235).

The second great crisis of Roman imperial civilization had been long in building—since the time of Marcus Aurelius—but now the defenses that Septimius Severus had hastily thrown up against social and political chaos crumbled. The mainstay of those defenses, the army, was the instrument of their destruction. Between A.D. 235 and 285 some thirty military commanders, adventurers, political opportunists, and outright criminals vied for the imperial office. During this period of civil strife, the frontiers disintegrated; barbarian tribes pierced the Roman confines; cities were sacked, abandoned, or proclaimed their independence from Rome; slaves rebelled or fled the great estates; pestilence struck; and all sense of civic responsibility disappeared. Taxation and conscription increased; population decreased; land fell into disuse and reverted to desert or swamp; barbarians rose to high command in the legions;

and in many places the money economy was supplanted by exchanges in kind. Only gradually, largely through the efforts of a number of talented soldiers from Illyria, especially Claudius Gothicus (268–270) and Aurelian (270–275), was order restored. But it was not by any means an order that was consistent with the ideas of either the republic or the Augustan Empire. The ordering principle that the Illyrians brought to the Roman world was oriental, more like that of ancient Egypt than that of either Greece or Rome.

THE ORIENTALIZATION OF ROME

The reforms undertaken by Diocletian (285–305) and Constantine the Great (305–337) completed the process of transformation that the political and social crises of the third century had made necessary for the empire. What had begun as a program designed to bring peace and prosperity to the entire Mediterranean world had ended as a program designed to ensure the mere survival of the Roman state, at any price. The power wielded by the emperors was no longer regarded as finding its justification in the promotion of the "good life" originally encouraged by it, but was openly proclaimed as a hard necessity. Although Diocletian tried to provide an ideological justification for his power by importing the kind of emperor-worship that had flourished in Egypt since the time of the pharaohs, it was manifest that the empire was no longer considered to be a means to an end, but as an end in itself. The citizens of the empire were now called upon to sacrifice everything— their wealth, their property, their lives, even their consciences—for the preservation of the state.

Thus the distinction between the "good life" envisioned by Greek and Roman humanism and the "mere life" of the barbarian disappeared. More and more barbarian tribes were settled within the confines of the empire and permitted to maintain their older, tribal ways as long as they paid their taxes and provided troops for the legions. The army itself was gradually barbarized and turned into an instrument of sheer oppression, the main task of which was to maintain the authority of tax collectors and other bureaucrats. The older social mobility was supplanted by a caste system, as Diocletian froze membership in certain classes and professions to assure the performance of those duties deemed essential to the life of the empire. Taxes were assessed without any consideration of the individual's ability to pay; duties were assigned without any thought of the individual's ability to carry them out. The empire as a whole was divided into units reflecting the willingness of the emperors to abandon whatever could not carry its own weight in the general endeavor.

In short, Roman society now became divided, both geographically and socially, into those parts worth saving and those worthy only of being exploited. Expressed geographically, this meant that if necessity required, the western part of the empire, the agrarian part, would be abandoned in favor of the eastern, or commercial, part. Socially, it meant that any group not contributing directly to the maintenance of the imperial bureaucracy or army would be sacrificed. What had started out as a government of service to an ideal, ended as a government of subjection to the "realities" of life. The result was to alienate most of the populace, and when the barbarians finally swept into the western portions of the empire, they were just as often welcomed as liberators as they were opposed as oppressors.

Those Romans who did not openly join the barbarians, showed their alienation by adopting a world-view completely opposed to everything for which classical materialism had stood—that of Christianity. By the end of Diocletian's reign, Christianity was the single largest religious community within the Roman world. It was openly hostile to the ideal of Greek humanism and the institutions of the Roman empire. It was a master stroke on Constantine's part to make Christianity the favored religion of the empire in A.D. 313. By doing so, he not only neutralized the Christian clergy, he found a way of enlisting the lower classes of the empire in a program of self-abnegating service even more demanding than that projected by Diocletian.

It was already apparent by the end of Diocletian's reign that the emperor-worship imported from Egypt could not provide the ideological cement for the military autocracy he headed. The oriental religions in general appealed to a principle of material self-interest, which was as harmful to the sense of community in adversity as classical humanism itself had been. Basically, all of the oriental religions played upon men's fear of death; they promised them some kind of salvation but made them apathetic with respect to the here and now, and, in the process, something less than dedicated servants of the general social interest. It was difficult for any enlightened man to believe the sustaining myths of the oriental mystery cults, and the unenlightened men usually could not gain access to them. Moreover, it mattered little to the lower classes whether the emperor was the incarnated sun-god or not, since his beneficence did not shine upon them in either case.

Therefore, when Constantine decided to abandon the emperor's claim to divinity and embrace Christianity, he was not giving up very much. But in return he received a great deal that was beneficial to the state. First of all, Christianity taught that the principal human virtue was charity, respect for and service to one's neighbors. It taught that life on earth was necessarily painful and hard, but, while it pointed men's attention to the eternal life that awaited beyond the grave, it held that this eternal life had to be won here on earth, through acts of charity to one's neighbors and foes alike. It therefore made of the quest for salvation, which obsessed the late Roman world, a *communal* quest above all. Every man was responsible for his own salvation, to be sure; but he could not win that salvation without serving his fellowman.

Secondly, Christianity offered the benefits claimed by all of the other oriental religions to everyone, regardless of race, sex, social status, or degree of intellectual enlightenment. Jesus could be interpreted as an incarnated god, as moral paragon, or as simply a great teacher—but he was above all *the* man, the type of humanity in its perfect form, the man-god. All men participated in that humanity to some degree and could win a similar divinity if they willed to do so. Christianity was exclusivistic in its insistence that its devotees renounce all other religions, but it was broadly tolerant in its willingness to accept any man or woman into its community. It thus could be seen as mirroring the universalism of the empire itself.

Finally, Christianity possessed an exceptionally well-organized administrative body, the clergy, whose strength rested on the democratic nature of its election. From the local groups presided over by a priest up through bishops and metropolitans, the clergy represented a chain of authority that was grounded in the loyalty of the individual believer. It had its own methods of discipline (excommunication) and its own instrument for coordinating policy (the councils). It might have appeared, as it had appeared earlier, to be a kind of state within the state, had it not been for the fact that the clergy did not aspire to political power and were content to leave political power to the Caesars, if they could carry out their religions duties as they saw fit. What Constantine did was to weld this exceptionally stable and resilient religious community onto the Roman state and use it as a base for a new conception of the imperial office as God's vicegerency on earth, after the Mesopotamian, rather than the Egyptian, model of kingship.

This is not to suggest that the fourth-century emperors were merely cynical exploiters of Christianity for political purposes. Christianity was the largest single religion in the empire; it was well organized; and it inculcated an ideal of self-abnegating social service that could be turned to political use. In a time of war, invasion, pestilence, or economic decline, it steeled men's resolution. And it made them good citizens insofar as the ends of the state could be interpreted as Christian ends. Constantine's adoption of Christianity signaled the bankruptcy of classical humanism as a political creed. It represented the abandonment of what C. N. Cochrane called "the religion of culture" in favor of the new "culture of religion." It was less a betrayal of humanistic ideals than a realistic recognition of a process of disintegration that had been going on within classical culture itself since the end of the first century.

THE DECLINE OF CLASSICAL HUMANISM

The Augustan Empire had professed to give men what the Greek *polis* had only promised them—that is, a stable social world within which the quest for selfhood could be pursued in maximum security. Effectively, it asked men to give up control over their political destinies in return for that material plenty without which the good life could not be achieved. The arrangement presupposed a kind of social middle ground between the individual and the state on which the individual could give public expression to his talents and abilities. As long as this social middle ground remained relatively open and flexible—as it did through the period of the "five good emperors"—the empire proved more than adequate. But as the state became increasingly hard pressed to provide the material resources for its own legitimate activities—maintenance of the army, care of the indigent lower classes, defense of the frontiers, and the like—it was forced as a result to restrict the areas of expression formerly available to the free individual in society. Gradually, larger and larger areas of the social life were removed as fields wherein individual initiative and achievement might be expressed. Thus the provincial cities were turned into little more than tax-collecting stations, the landed estates into tax-producing units, and the community of free men, which had existed between the slave populace on the one hand and the imperial court and bureaucracy on the other, into a regimented army of tax merchants. Those who could not meet the demands laid upon them were reduced to slavery or outlawry. Those who did meet them found little satisfaction in the performance of their duties, since, whatever they did, it was never sufficient to the needs of the increasingly harassed and growing state mechanism.

In short, the Augustan settlement was essentially a fair-weather solution to the problem of human community in the ancient world. It tacitly assumed that the material resources on which the social order was based would remain constant and adequate to the needs of the state. Within the limits of that assumption it delivered what it promised, but when the material resources of the empire—land, manpower, and markets—declined, the emperors were forced to try to create wealth by arbitrarily redefining what men were entitled to want or desire. In the situation that had developed by the end of the second century A.D. one of the items that had to be classed as luxury was any form of public expression that did not contribute to the well-being of the army or the bureaucracy. Thus the notion of what constituted the good life was progressively restricted, until in the end the "good life" was not distinguishable from service to the state.

The question thus arises, Why did the Romans feel compelled to redefine the good life in the face of material decline rather than try to discover the causes of material decline and take some action to promote a recovery? The answer lies partially in the conception of nature that dominated the whole of ancient thought. As noted in our discussion of Greek humanism, classical science assumed that the world was fixed in its essential aspects. The problem of human thought was to discover the principles informing nature and thereby make *adjustment* to its processes easier. Anyone who did not want to adjust to the world as thus conceived might entertain hope of escaping from it into some ideal sphere of spirit, pure mind, or perfect form; but the world itself was not believed to be reformable.

The same fatalism prevailed in classical political and social thought. Here it was assumed that the only perfect order that could ever exist had existed in the remote past; perfect order was not possible in the present or future. Hence political reform was never conceived as innovation but always as renovation, a return to the first principles. It was therefore very difficult to imagine a fundamental reordering of the political sphere in the interest of a new kind of life. All one could do in a crisis was try to save whatever one could of the old order.

Similarly, it was impossible to imagine undertaking scientific experiments to increase the yield of the soil or to increase population growth; one could only adjust to nature's imperious commands and make the best of it. Thus the pessimism that emanated from senatorial literary circles during the first century A.D. was ultimately justified—because pessimism can always be justified at some time in the long run. Senatorial pessimism was not based upon a genuine understanding of the forces at work in the Roman empire or the weaknesses of Caesarism. The best that the most sophisticated critics of Caesarism could propose as an alternative to the *status quo* was a return to "the good old ways" of the republic.

Hegel notes that in the late stages of a civilization, *talk* about virtue tends to take the place of virtuous acts. This aphorism might serve as the epitaph for Roman thought during the imperial period. The Stoic philosopher Seneca (4 B.C.–A.D. 65), teacher and guardian of Nero, represents most perfectly the disparity between thought and action during imperial times. There is no reason to doubt the sincerity of his *desire* to live an austere and disciplined life; the dignity with which he faced the death to which Nero condemned him confirms the nobility of his impulses. Nevertheless, he was constantly giving way to the temptations that offered themselves to him in the court of the tyrant.

Similarly, the historian Tacitus (A.D. 55–116), writing in the aftermath of Domitian's persecution of the senatorial aristocracy, finds nothing but vice in his own lived present and nothing but virtue in the republican past. But he is unable to imagine any way of returning to the earlier, purer age. He seems bleakly reconciled to living in an age of decadence, and he takes a perverse pleasure in chronicling the virtues of the savage Germans, who, in his view at least, have the advantage of a happy ignorance. Like Rousseau later on, he finds social existence itself debilitating, though he can conceive no possible alternative to the *status quo*.

In the atmosphere of political terrorism that Domitian had created, it was inevitable that thought follow one of three lines: resentful chronicling of the evils of the time, mere gossip, or ironic acceptance of the world with all its shortcomings. Tacitus represents the first course, Pliny the Younger (62–*ca.* 114) the second, and the satirists Juvenal (flourished *ca.* A.D. 100) and Martial (*ca.* 40–*ca.* 104) the third. In no case was there any advancement of a genuine alternative to the prevalent practices.

During the imperial period, Roman social thought manifested everywhere an accommodative spirit, a resigned acceptance of the inevitable. It shows us men regarding the world as sliding into a tired old-age and a decision to take what pleasures life offered before all pleasures were withdrawn. Even the Stoic emperor Marcus Aurelius could offer little more than a kind of stage-director's ethic: one did one's duty because one had been consigned one's task by fate. The idea that one might rewrite the script of world history or change the stage setting was utterly alien to him.

It is easy to see why, in this atmosphere, a philosophy like that of Plato might appeal to many of the better educated. The Neo-Platonism of the imperial period taught that the material world was irredeemable and advised men to abandon it to its own devices and seek salvation in the pursuit of the changeless, eternal spiritual realm. As articulated by Plotinus (205–270), Neo-Platonism undermined Roman concern for serious attention to political and social problems. It taught that the material sphere was a dream and defined full awakening of the soul as a flight from the material world to union with the changeless sphere of pure spirit, beyond time and space. It was aristocratic and elitist, making salvation dependent upon learning, and virtue synonymous with disinterest in the problems of one's fellowmen.

It can, therefore, be easily understood why, by the beginning of the third century, men everywhere were abandoning the conventional classical approaches to individual self-definition in favor of Christianity. Stoicism demanded an impossible self-discipline in the face of a social order that perversely undermined rather than aided any attempt at responsible public activity; Epicureanism taught abandonment of the self to immediate pleasure in the face of a closing-off of most forms of enjoyment; Neo-Platonism taught a flight from the world that was little more than metaphysical suicide.

Christianity by contrast taught the possibility of a new beginning, for individual men and for the whole world. It allowed men to believe that history could begin anew— had begun anew with the coming of the Savior. While viewing the world as governed by a just and all-powerful God, while affirming that men necessarily suffered from their very humanity, and while admitting that all fundamental transformations of the world had to originate with God alone, Christianity required of men that they act *as if* they had within themselves real control over their capacities for good and evil. Moreover, while demanding the highest kind of moral rectitude of the individual, it recognized the possibility that the individual might from time to time fail in the execution of his good intentions, without excluding the possibility of yet another beginning and another winning of the eternal life offered by Jesus to every man.

The Greco-Roman conception of human personality was as substantialist as its conception of the world at large. It held that the individual was given a finite fund of talent and virtue at birth, and it defined the individual life-process as the full realization of that talent and virtue. Any failure to realize to the full the potential contained in the primal fund was regarded as tragic, but it was not assumed that the fund could be renewed or extended beyond the time given by fate.

Christianity taught that life was a testing ground where, if men chose to, they could draw upon an infinite fund of creative potential (grace), which could be utilized even beyond the grave. It taught that virtuous acts were better than any amount of virtuous talk, that virtuous thought was a necessary preliminary to virtuous actions, and that any man who seriously willed it could attain to an immortality that had hitherto been vouchsafed only to the gods. Moreover, while admitting that the material world was "a snare and a delusion," Christianity still maintained that the world was not in itself evil; it was only the neutral stage upon which God had chosen to produce the drama of salvation. For the Christian, the world was a *means* of salvation. At the same time, other human beings had to be treated as ends in themselves, as cherished by God, and therefore as cherishable by other men. Through service to other men, the individual man might put off his animal nature and assume a new existence, one that was not limited by time and space, but was eternal, and eternally joyous. Thus, while keeping men's attention riveted constantly to the world beyond, Christianity permitted a creative confrontation of the world immediately given to human consciousness and held it up as a challenge, which men avoided at their everlasting peril.

The preparation for Christianity's reception among the cultivated classes of the Roman empire had been going on since the end of the first century. From an original hostility to the world in all its aspects, Christians had turned increasingly to a realization of the socially responsible implications of the doctrine of charity. The apologist Justin Martyr (second century A.D.) had shown how the Christian doctrine could be reconciled with the moral teachings of Socrates and the metaphysical ideas of Plato. And while the "puritan" Tertullian (ca. 160–ca. 230) had remained adamant in his hostility to both reason and the political sphere—asking "What is Athens to Jerusalem?" and answering, "Nothing"—the Christian Bishop Cyprian (A.D. ca. 200–258) had provided a new, communal message as an antidote to excessive individualism, a willingness to forgive backsliding in place of a puritan demand for perfect saintliness in men, and a reconciliation of the church with the state if the state itself showed any inclination to put off the old pagan ways and put on the new Christian ones.

All of this reached its culmination in the late fourth century, when a group of remarkable churchmen, trained in classical thought but converted to Christian ideals, showed how Christianity could be regarded, not as a negation alone, but also as a fulfillment of classical ideals of humanity and community. St. Ambrose of Milan (ca. 340–397) brought a mind trained in law to his analysis of the nature of the church and its relations to the state. And St. Augustine of Hippo (354–430) brought a mind trained in philosophy and rhetoric to his consideration of the meaning of Rome's dissolution. The Roman Empire, he wrote in the *City of God*, had been allowed to flourish to show the extent to which men could progress on their own abilities alone. Its decline could be understood in terms similar to those that made the sufferings of the Jews understandable. The lesson to be learned from the fall of Rome was unequivocal: without God's help neither natural human strength nor natural human virtue could prevail. With God's help both the state and the individual could thrive, the former providing protection for men while the message of the Gospels was being proclaimed throughout the world, the latter spreading that message, by deeds as well as by words. On this earth, the state and the church found their strength in one another. At the end of the world-process, however, the state would wither away, to be replaced by the true community of saints, each living a perfect, individual life in direct communion with the one, eternal God.

SELECTED
BIBLIOGRAPHY

This bibliography is limited mainly to literature available in paperback editions. However, since many of the numerous books on ancient Greece and Rome are not available in paperback, a few of the most essential ones are included here. These are indicated by an asterisk.

Students doing research on any aspect of either Greek or Roman life will find two reference works invaluable: *The Oxford Classical Dictionary** (Oxford: At the Clarendon Press, 1953) and the multivolumed *Cambridge Ancient History** (Cambridge: Cambridge University Press, 1923–1939). There are in addition a host of handbooks, dictionaries, and compendia dealing with specific aspects of the classical world, from myth and religion to science and philosophy. In general, however, the student will find a wealth of brief popularizations of scholarly work on the ancients in the paperback literature. The following lists, organized by topics, represent only a fraction of titles at the student's disposal.

GREEK POLITICAL AND SOCIAL HISTORY

AGARD, WALTER R. *What Democracy Meant to the Greeks* (University of Wisconsin Press, 1960). A study of the origins of Greek thinking about the concept of democracy, locating it in traditional Greek culture, comparing it to modern ideas on the subject, and criticizing its weaknesses.

ANDREWES, A. *Greek Tyrants* (Harper Torchbooks, 1963). A brief, excellent study of the popular leaders and strong men of the Greek city-states, anecdotal and colorful.

BOWRA, C. M. *Periclean Athens* (Dial Press, 1971). A history of Athens in the fifth century B.C. by one of the deans of modern classical studies, stressing the relationship between Athenian democracy and imperialism.

FORSDYKE, JOHN. *Greece Before Homer* (Norton, 1957). Using archeological and literary evidence, the author tries to reconstruct the thought-world of the earliest Greeks; should be interesting to those fascinated by the problem of dating and documentation of preliterate cultures.

FREEMAN, KATHLEEN. *Greek City States* (Norton, 1963). A study of nine Greek city-states with the exception of Athens and Sparta, heavily dependent on archeological evidence and stressing the influence of geographical factors on their evolution.

KAGAN, DONALD. *Outbreak of the Peloponnesian War* (Cornell, 1969). A fresh interpretation of the problem by a leading young American classicist.

MITCHELL, H. *Sparta* (Cambridge University Press, 1952). The product of a lifetime of scholarship, purporting to relate every known fact about Spartan development, especially strong on economic and political history.

ROSTOVTZEFF, MICHAEL. *Greece*, edited by Elias J. Bickerman (Galaxy Books, 1963). Originally published in 1926, this book by one of the masters of ancient history offers an anti-Marxist, though economic, interpretation of Greek development.

SMITH, MORTON. *Ancient Greeks* (Cornell, 1960). Deals with

social, political, and cultural developments from the eleventh to the third century B.C.

ZIMMER, ALFRED. *The Greek Commonwealth: Politics and Economics in Fifth Century Athens* (Galaxy Books, 1961). Originally published in 1911, Zimmer's classic study of ancient Athens has been superseded by more recent scholarship, but the interpretation is profound and the analogies drawn between ancient and modern political atomism are compelling even today.

GREEK MYTH AND RELIGION

CORNFORD, F. M. *From Religion to Philosophy: A Study in the Origins of Western Speculation* (Harper Torchbooks, 1957). A brilliant work by one of the most profound of classical scholars; written before World War I, this work demonstrates the essentially mythical structure of Greek philosophy without suggesting that it is less important for being "mythic."

COULANGES, FUSTEL DE. *Ancient City* (Anchor Books, 1956). A classic work on the classic age, rich in speculative insights and anticipations of later, cultural-anthropological and even psychoanalytical, insights. Much of the data has been superseded, so this book must be used with caution; but it is a mine of brilliant generalizations that could be used as topics for research.

DODDS, E. R. *The Greeks and the Irrational* (Beacon, 1957). An examination of Greek attitudes towards magic, the gods, the psyche, shamanism, worship, and so on, illuminated by cultural-anthropological and psychoanalytic theories.

GRANT, MICHAEL. *Myths of the Greeks and Romans* (Mentor, 1962). A catalogue of the principal Greek and Roman myths and interpretations of their significance; with extensive bibliography for further study.

GRAVES, ROBERT. *Greek Myths*, 2 vols. (Penguin, 1957). An idiosyncratic retelling of many of the main Greek myths by a talented British poet, in dictionary form.

GUTHRIE, W. K. C. *The Greeks and their Gods* (Beacon, 1955). Meant to be a kind of companion to the reading of the

Greek classics, this book explicates the Greeks' conception of their relationship to the gods and ends with a discussion of the theologies of Plato and Aristotle.

HARRISON, JANE E. *Prolegomena to the Study of Greek Religion* (Meridian, 1955). Originally published in 1903, this was an epoch-making work, reflecting the impact of what was then the new science of anthropology; thick and difficult, but worthy of study today.

MURRAY, GILBERT. *The Five Stages of Greek Religion* (Anchor Books, 1955). Another classic in the field, published originally in 1912. In the tradition of Harrison's study, but clearer and more easily comprehended.

OTTO, WALTER F. *Homeric Gods: The Spiritual Significance of Greek Religions* (Beacon, 1954). Treats Greek religion as a serious theological position, rather than as a curiosity; illuminates Greek thought and literature as well as myth.

GREEK PHILOSOPHY, HISTORIOGRAPHY, AND SCIENCE

ARMSTRONG, A. H. *Introduction to Ancient Philosophy* (Beacon, 1963). A comprehensive survey of the history of Greek thought from the earliest times to that of St. Augustine; stresses the Greek contribution to the later Thomistic synthesis of the Middle Ages.

BURNET, JOHN. *Early Greek Philosophy* (Meridian, 1957). Originally published in 1892, this work is still the standard interpretation of the pre-Socratic texts.

BURY, J. B. *Ancient Greek Historians* (Dover, 1958). Another classic of interpretation, originally published in 1908, dealing with the rise of Greek historiography in Ionia, with extended treatments of Herodotus, Thucydides, and Polybius.

COPLESTON, FREDERICK. *History of Philosophy*, vol. 1 (Anchor Books, 1962). A standard modern history of ancient philosophy, stressing the historical context as well as the doctrines of the principal thinkers.

CORNFORD, F. M. *Before and After Socrates* (Cambridge, 1960).

A fine introduction to the Ionian thinkers and to Socrates, Plato, and Aristotle; old but good.

FARRINGTON, BENJAMIN. *Greek Science* (Penguin, 1949). An excellent work by a prominent dialectical materialist.

FINLEY, M. I., ed. *The Portable Greek Historians* (Viking, 1959). Texts of the major Greek historians, prefaced by a fine introductory essay by a major interpreter of Greek thought.

GREENE, WILLIAM C. *Moira: Fate, Good and Evil in Greek Thought* (Harper Torchbooks, 1963). A study of the Greek conception of fate, from Homer to Euripides; somewhat abstract at times but illuminating of many areas of Greek culture.

GRUBE, G. M. A. *Plato's Thought* (Beacon, 1958). A study of the dialogues.

FRIEDLÄNDER, PAUL. *Plato: An Introduction* (Harper Torchbooks, 1964). The first volume of a three-volume work, discussing the historical context of Plato's thought.

NEEDHAM, JOSEPH, ed. *Background to Modern Science* (Cambridge University Press, 1930). Ten lectures on Greek natural philosophy and modern science, tracing the connections between the two.

RANDALL, JOHN HERMAN. *Aristotle* (Columbia University Press, 1960). One of the major naturalistic philosophers of contemporary America discusses the Greek philosopher closest to him in spirit.

ROSS, W. D. *Aristotle* (Meridian, 1959). A short commentary on Aristotle's main works, with an especially helpful discussion of his *Logic*.

SAUVAGE, MICHELENE. *Socrates and the Human Conscience* (Harper Torchbooks, 1961). Deals with later European philosophers' conceptions of Socrates and with the principal ideas of Socrates.

SNELL, BRUNO. *The Discovery of the Mind: Greek Origins of European Thought* (Harper Torchbooks, 1960). An analysis of the main themes of Greek thought and its impact on the European cultural tradition.

TAYLOR, A. E. *Aristotle* (Dover, 1956). Originally published in 1919, still one of the best short introductions to Aristotle's thought in English.

————. *Plato: The Man and his Work* (Meridian, 1956). A companion to Plato's dialogues, setting the topic of each within the historical context it alludes to.

TOYNBEE, ARNOLD J. *Greek Historical Thought* (Mentor, 1952). Selections and assessments of the main Greek historians, by a great philosopher of history of our time.

GREEK LITERATURE

BOWRA, C. M. *Greek Lyric Poetry* (Oxford, 1936). A useful introduction by a master classicist.

BURN, A. R. *The Lyric Age of Greece* (Arnold, 1960). Concentrates on the seventh and sixth centuries B.C., relating poetic style to Greek life in that age.

COCHRANE, C. N. *Christianity and Classical Culture* (Galaxy, 1960). A brilliant synthesis of the literary, philosophical, religious, and political strains of classical culture in the transition time between Homer and St. Augustine. Although dealing primarily with the Roman-Christian period, it contains valuable work on the Greek heritage.

EHRENBERG, VICTOR. *People of Aristophanes: A Sociology of Old Attic Comedy* (Schocken, 1962). Uses Old Attic comedy as source for a reconstruction of the social world of Athens; also utilizes archeological and epigraphical evidence.

————. *Sophocles and Pericles* (Oxford, 1954). Sets the life of fifth-century Athens within the context of a consideration of the careers of its greatest dramatist and its most brilliant statesman.

JAEGER, WERNER. *Paideia*, 3 vols. *(Blackwell, 1939). A major interpretation of the ideals of Greek culture conceived as a basis for a general theory of human development through "education" (*paideia*).

KITTO, H. D. F. *Greek Tragedy* (Anchor, 1955). A good introduction to a complex subject, written in a clear style by a major student of Greek literature.

LATTIMORE, RICHMOND. *Story Patterns in Greek Tragedy* (University of Michigan Press, 1969). Not an outline of the plays, but an analysis of fundamental plot-structures, by a brilliant translator of the classics.

MURRAY, GILBERT. *The Rise of the Greek Epic* (Galaxy, 1960).
    Sets the Greek epic within its religious and historical
    context.

GREEK ART

GROENEWEGEN-FRANKFORT, H. A., and ASHMOLE, BERNARD. *The
    Ancient World*. Vol. I of The Library of Art History
    (Mentor, 1967). An original and comprehensive survey
    of ancient art, setting the Greek and Roman achievements
    within the context of developments throughout the
    Mediterranean; containing an extensive bibliography.
HAUSER, ARNOLD. *The Social History of Art*, vols. 1 and 2.
    (Vintage, 1957–1958). A controversial, because it is a
    Marxist, interpretation of the history of art; suggestive
    and stimulating.

HELLENISTIC CULTURE

Students will find discussions of the transition period
between Greek and Roman history in the standard surveys
of both; but two works can be consulted profitably.

TARN, W. W. *Alexander the Great* (Beacon, 1956). A study of
    Alexander and his plan for the "unification of mankind";
    both a biography of Alexander and history of his ideals.
————. *Hellenistic Civilization* (Meridian, 1961). A superb
    short introduction, attempting to define the general pat-
    tern of the culture of the period.

ROMAN POLITICS AND SOCIAL INSTITUTIONS

BARROW, R. H. *The Romans* (Penguin, 1962). Originally written
    in 1931 by a distinguished classicist, this book was sub-
    stantially rewritten in the 1940s.
COWELL, F. R. *Cicero and the Roman Republic* (Penguin, 1956).
    Deals with Roman life in society, culture, and politics as

reflected in the life and career of Cicero; a comprehensive study.

GIBBON, EDWARD. *Decline and Fall of the Roman Empire.* There are many editions of this great classic, which deals with the fate of Greco-Roman culture from the time of the Antonines to the fall of Constantinople (1453). Students may want to consult the abridged version in *The Portable Gibbon* (Viking, 1952).

HAMMOND, MASON. *City State and World State** (Harvard University Press, 1951).

MOMMSEN, THEODORE. *History of Rome* (Meridian, 1958). Originally published in 1889, this is the work of the greatest classical historian of the nineteenth century.

MATTINGLY, H. *Roman Imperial Civilization* (Anchor, 1959). Primarily a political account of Roman civilization, with only side references to other aspects of Roman life; shows how Roman government worked.

ROSTOVTZEFF, MICHAEL. *Rome* (Galaxy, 1960). A popular version of the great Roman historian's conception of Rome's rise and fall; originally published in 1927.

————. *The Social and Economic History of the Roman Empire** (Oxford, 1926). The masterpiece of one of the twentieth century's most imaginative classical historians; argues in what appears to be a class analysis of Roman growth and decline that, ultimately, the Empire was simply swamped by barbarians from below.

SCULLARD, H. H. *From the Gracchi to Nero* (Praeger, 1959). An exceedingly complete and comprehensive survey of Roman political and institutional development from the end of the Punic Wars to the middle of the first century A. D.

SYME, RONALD. *The Roman Revolution* (Oxford, 1960). Written during the days before World War II, this book interprets the Augustan settlement in something less than sympathetic terms, seeing in it a form of "totalitarianism" that subverted the Republic; accounts of the culture of the Augustan age, especially as reflected in Virgil and Livy, are especially interesting.

WHEELER, M. *Rome Beyond Imperial Frontiers* (Pelican, 1955). Deals with Roman trade and foreign policy with respect to Africa, Asia, and Europe.

ROMAN CULTURE AND CIVILIZATION

ADCOCK, F. E. *Roman Political Ideas and Practice* (University of Michigan Press, 1959). Traces development of Roman political practices and changes in Roman political ideas and ideals, from the Monarchy to the Principate; deals with the Roman voting system in detail.

DAVENPORT, BASIL, ed. *The Portable Roman Reader* (Viking, 1951). An anthology of seven centuries of Roman cultural life and history, with selections from historians, dramatists, poets, and so on.

GRANT, MICHAEL. *World of Rome* (Mentor, 1960). Gives a picture of Rome at the height of its powers; dealing with political and social structure, religious ideals, and literature.

GRANT, FREDERICK C., ed. *Ancient Roman Religion* (Library of Liberal Arts, 1957). Documents of Roman religion from its "agricultural" phase to its defeat by Christianity in the last days of the Empire.

HADAS, MOSES, ed. *The Stoic Philosophy of Seneca* (Anchor, 1958). An excellent introduction to the thought of the most important Roman philosopher.

MACKENDRICK, PAUL. *The Roman Mind at Work* (Anvil, 1958). An analysis of the Roman ways of dealing with practical problems, such as war, trade, slavery, and so on, followed by a set of well-chosen documents illustrative of the general principles outlined in the introduction.

ROSE, H. J. *Handbook of Latin Literature* (Everyman, 1958). A discussion of the development of Latin literature from the earliest times to the death of St. Augustine, with a bibliography brought up to date as of 1966.

STARR, CHESTER G. *Civilization and the Caesars** (Cornell, 1954). A study of the evolution of culture and its relation to political developments during the Empire. Can be read in profitable conjunction with Cochrane's *Christianity and Classical Culture* cited above, under "Greek Literature."

INDEX

Achilles, 26–27
  as ideal hero, 19–20
Actium, Battle of, 103
Aeneid, 116–117
Aeschylus, 63
Agammemnon, 26–27
Agrippa, Marcus, 103
Agrippina II, 124
Alexander the Great, 45, 81–
  82
  as creator of Hellenistic civ-
    ilization, 46–47
  divinization of, 45–46
  as enemy of polis, 46
  as student of Aristotle, 44,
    70
Ambrose, St., 142
Anaximander, 50
Anaximenes, 50
Antigone, 62–63
Antigonus, 46
Antiochus, 86
Antoninus Pius, 128
Antony, Mark, 103–104
Aristotle, 44
  anti-idealism of, 69

as influence on Hellenistic
  thought, 71
political philosophy of, 70
Athens
  Cleisthenes's reform of, 35–
    36
  decline of, 43–44
  and Delian League, 40
  golden age of, 39–41
  and Peloponnesian Wars,
    41–44
  Pisistratus's reforms of, 35
  resistance to Persia of, 37–
    38
  Solon's reform of, 35
  as type of *polis,* 32–33
Auctoritas, Roman conception
  of, 93–95
Auerbach, Erich, cited on
  Greek epic, 21
Augustine, St., 78, 120, 142
  and Neo-Platonism, 78
Augustus
  and Agrippa, 103–104
  cultural reforms of, 108,
    115–117
  death of, 119

153